CROSSEYED

HOW TO HAVE VICTORY OVER SIN

MICHAEL CHOREY

Cross-Eyed

Second Edition
ISBN: 978-1-945423-02-4
Copyright © 2016, 2014 Mike Chorey

Front & Back Cover Design by Aaron McClung
Interior Redesign by Randall E. Johnson

A publication of Joshua Revolution
716.284.8173

P.O. Box 923
Grand Island, NY 14072
www.joshuarevolution.org

Published through the
International Localization Network
and
5 Stones Publishing
109 Sunset Court #2
Hamburg, NY 14075

Formerly:
Elim Publishing
1679 Dalton Rd
Lima, NY 14485

Printed in the United States of America

CROSS-EYED

How To Have Victory Over Sin

One of the most important questions that the child of God can ask is, "How do I live in victory over sin?" This book is designed to give you the biblical answer and to lead you into spiritual freedom. Our prayer is that as you find the answer, you will teach others the pathway of victory prescribed in the Bible!

"And the things that thou hast heard of me among many witnesses, the same commit thou to faithful men, who shall be able to teach others also" (II Timothy 2:2).

Written by Michael Chorey

Contents

Introduction

There is no greater moment in a person's life than when he comes to faith in Jesus Christ and is "born of the Spirit" (John 3:3). When the Holy Spirit convicts a person of his sins (Acts 2:37), that person acknowledges his sins (I John 1:9), he repents, and he places his faith in Jesus Christ. What does it mean to repent of sin? Repentance means acknowledging that you are a sinner, asking the Lord's forgiveness for your wrongs, and consciously deciding to stop knowingly committing wrongdoing (Acts 2:38). Also, you put your faith in Jesus Christ and what Jesus did for you personally on the Cross to atone for (pardon) your sins (Ephesians 2:8-9). At that moment of confessing that you are a sinner, asking the Lord to enter your heart, and turning from sinful ways, the Holy Spirit comes into your life. This is what the Bible calls being "born again" (John 3:3).

After receiving Christ as Savior (John 1:12), the next important step is to go on with Christ and learn how to walk in victory over sin so our lives please God and glorify Him. That is one of the main reasons we have the Bible—so we can know how to live a life pleasing to God. If believers do not know how to live for God, we will continue to go back to our sinful ways. The devil is a thief; he knows that he can steal the Word from the new believer (Mark 4:15), and keep the believer in a state of failure. Therefore, we need to learn what the Word teaches to keep us walking in the Lord's ways in order to have victory over sin. The Word is full of hope, encouragement, and instruction in the ways of faith in Christ Jesus. We can break the cycle of sinning and repenting, sinning and repenting – there is victory over sin! We can overcome the frustrations in "trying" to live the Christian life and experience the "abundant life" that Jesus promises to those who believe in Him.

The thief cometh not, but for to steal, and to kill, and to destroy: I am come that they might have life, and that they might have it more abundantly.

John 10:10

Cross-Eyed

Statistics tell us today that one of every two Christian marriages ends in divorce. In fact, Christian marriages are failing at the same rate as non-Christian marriages. Why? We could say that many people who are calling themselves Christians have never been truly "born again." But I also believe it is because many Christians—although they love God and don't want to fail God—are living the defeated Christian life. Although they look to the Cross for salvation, they do not look to the Cross for victorious living. If Christians do not properly understand what Jesus accomplished through His death on the Cross, they are left helpless to fight the temptations of the world.

It is critically important that every believer understands the pathway to victory over sin. The Bible has not left us directionless. In fact, almost 98% of the New Testament gives instruction about how to live for God once we are saved.

It is my prayerful intention that this book, which will take you on a step-by-step journey of the revelation of the Cross, will completely inform you of how to defeat the powers of darkness and how to be freed from the bondage of sin. This careful look at what the Bible teaches is going to bring your faith back to where it was on the day that you got saved! Once believers receive this revelation, which was first given to Paul, they are going to feel as though they have been born again—again!

ONE FINAL COMMENT BEFORE WE BEGIN

Remember, the Bible does not only command us to read the Bible, but it commands us to study the Bible. Second Timothy 2:15 says, "Study to shew thyself approved unto God, a workman that needeth not to be ashamed, rightly dividing the word of truth." Therefore I encourage you not to just read *Cross-Eyed,* but to use it to help you study the Word.

Chapter One
My Personal Testimony

I got saved on Sunday, March 28, 1982, at The Chapel on North Forest Road in Buffalo, New York. My sister had been sharing Christ with me for over a year. On the day I got saved, I knew something had changed. I walked down the aisle of the church to the altar and the pastor met me there and asked me *"Why have you come forward?"* I thought that if I answered this question wrong I may not get saved. I didn't know what to say, so I said the first thing that came to my mind. I said, *"Because I love Jesus."* He replied, *"That's the right answer."*

I repented of my sins and put my faith in Christ as my personal Savior that day. I knew when I walked that aisle that it was all for Jesus. I instantly became in love with the Word of God as the Holy Spirit came into my life and began to reveal the truths of the Scriptures to me.

A few years later, I was wonderfully filled with the Holy Spirit one day after football practice, while attending the University at Buffalo. A few months after my encounter with the Holy Spirit, the Lord called me into full-time ministry. I joined the ministry of Youth For Christ after college, and I started a brand new chapter in the Western New York area with the help of my sister and a good friend.

I worked with teenagers on the high school campuses, coaching football and telling students about Jesus. It was hard work. I remember thinking, *"This is the hardest thing I have ever done."* I had to go on a public school campus and try to win secular students to Jesus; all the while, it was illegal to preach Jesus on a public school campus. On top of all that, I was responsible for raising my own salary. There were many times I felt like quitting. But God wouldn't let me quit. One thing I knew, I was called; and when God calls you, quitting really isn't an option.

The Lord had given me a great vision to reach teenagers. I noticed that the more I did for the Lord, the spiritual attacks from the devil got stronger. Sometimes it got so intense and the oppression was so great, I didn't think I was going to make it. But the Spirit of the Lord always pulled me through.

The Lord started opening great doors for us to reach many young people with the Gospel. Through a Christmas Youth Conference, we were able to reach between five and six thousand students and leaders annually. The Lord gave us a weekly radio show where we were able to reach many more each week as well. We were doing evangelism on campuses, training youth leaders, running evangelistic meetings, crusades, and speaking to many people. God was using the ministry in a great way.

THEN THE DEVIL TURNED UP THE HEAT

But during this period, the devil began to turn up the heat. It was like the devil went before the Lord, just like he did with Job, and said, *"Lord if you let me go after Mike Chorey, I believe he will buckle and quit the ministry and stop following you."* I believe the Lord gave the devil permission but with certain restrictions (as would be obvious).

I began to notice that I was experiencing so much stress and oppression that I began to drift from the Lord. I got so defeated at one point, I thought I was going to leave the ministry altogether. I didn't understand why I felt so defeated. I was losing the desire to be in ministry, and at times, though they were few, I even had thoughts of leaving the Lord. Deep in my heart, I knew that following Jesus was the only true life for me, but I couldn't find the victory. I was a defeated Christian; my sin nature was ruling me; I felt like I was living a hypocritical life, and I was. I preached victory, but for a time it seemed like I only knew defeat.

During the worst times of my oppression, the Lord began to open the Cross to me. Even though I was trusting in what Jesus did on the Cross to save me from hell, I had never seen the Cross for victory over the power of my sin nature. I started to realize that, for most of my Christian life, I was living under a law mentality when it came to living for God. I was trying diligently to keep the Christian disciplines and even felt a sense of pride in my own commitment to the Lord. However, I really didn't know how the Holy Spirit worked. I thought that if I was faithful and disciplined, I wouldn't fall away.

But as I began to struggle in my walk with Jesus, I took a closer look at what Jesus had done at the Cross. I began to see the essence of my faith and how, on the Cross, Jesus not only paid for sin, He also broke the power of sin.

MY WRETCHED MAN MOMENT

Even though I knew it in my mind, I was still experiencing defeat in my Christian life. I knew the Lord wasn't happy with the way I was living, but I couldn't seem to break the hold the devil had on my life. I knew I was in the process of destroying everything, but I couldn't stop the downward slope I was on. One night after months of struggling, I came to the end of my rope. I cried out to the Lord with everything in me. Here were the words I said in desperation to the Lord as best as I can remember them.

"Lord, is this what Christianity is all about? You get saved, you get filled with the Holy Spirit, and you get called into the ministry…and then you become a failure and lose your way with God and quit the ministry. Is that what it is all about? Is the devil's power that strong?"

Then, in the midst of much weeping, the Lord brought to my mind the words of the Apostle Paul. In tears I cried out to the Lord with the same words of Paul that are found in Romans 7:24-25, *"O wretched man that I am! who shall deliver me from the body of this death? I thank God through Jesus Christ our Lord."*

As I laid there on the floor of my home, broken and ready to quit, the Lord began to move upon my heart. I sensed Him in a strong way! I knew the Lord caused a great breakthrough in my heart that night. I couldn't explain it, but I knew that God had broken the stronghold that the devil had on me. The next day, I felt like my sin nature had been pushed down. My desires to walk away from the ministry and the Lord were gone, and I had a new passion to live for God. The temptation of sin was gone. As the song says: *"Gone at last. My sins are gone at last. I was having a long streak of that bad, bad time, but now my sins, are gone at last!"*

Jesus Set Me Free!

The weeks and months that followed proved to me that something did happen the night that I cried out for the Lord to deliver me. The Scriptures about the Cross became even more eye-opening. The Lord began to show me what I was missing. I was living with spiritual pride, thinking that my walk was so strong with God that I could resist all the temptations of the devil. So the Lord allowed me to know how utterly helpless I am without His power. He showed me how much I needed Him and how, without the power of the Holy Spirit, I couldn't live the Christian life. I saw what a wretched man I really was and that I needed to depend on Him every moment of every day.

The River Started To Flow

From that time onward, the Lord started opening the Word of God to me and showing me the revelation of the Cross. It was like I got saved all over again. I was experiencing new joy and power in my walk with God. I just kept learning more and more about the Cross for godly living. It was like a river that just kept flowing stronger and stronger. In fact, to this day, that river just keeps getting deeper and deeper.

It's as if the Bible was a puzzle, and I had found the missing piece. Now everything in the Bible seemed to make greater sense to me as I began to see the Cross everywhere in Scripture.

Soon after the Lord gave me the revelation of the Cross, He called me to start a church. I put it off for several years because I didn't want to be a pastor. I just couldn't see myself behind the pulpit every week. I didn't want to deal with the endless problems that a pastor has to deal with.

But finally, after much confirmation and conviction that if we didn't start the church, I would be accountable to God someday for my disobedience, I realized I really didn't have a choice in the matter. So we opened the church in March of 2003.

From the moment the church opened, I knew why God had called me to it. He wanted me to give the Message of the Cross to as many people as possible. He gave me the victory and now He wanted me to teach others also. We even named the church according to the revelation the Lord had given me. We called it CrossRiver Church. It was the focus of the church to teach people that the flow of the River (the Holy Spirit) came through the revelation of the Cross. God was using me to build a church that was totally Cross-Eyed!

After experiencing the victory of the Cross for my personal sanctification (holy living), I started seeing our ministry experience a deeper anointing. More and more students were being saved, filled with the Spirit, and healed. The Message of the Cross, revealed to me through my desperate cry, was now being used to reach thousands of youths and adults.

THE DEVIL RETURNED

After a while, I noticed that I started struggling again. Even though it wasn't anything like it was before, still, I felt I was slowly slipping back into that hole from which I had been delivered. I couldn't understand why. Then I realized; the devil had left, but now he was back. The one thing I have learned about the devil— he never gives up trying.

But now I knew the Message of the Cross was the message of victory. I now knew how to resist the devil and what would cause him to flee. It was the blood and the dependence on the blood that was shed that the devil couldn't fight against.

However, even though the Lord had gloriously set me free from the power of my sin nature through this revelation, my sin nature was sticking up its ugly head again and giving me some problems. Even though it was nowhere near what it once was, I still was concerned and wondered why this was happening. I mean, I now knew the victory. I thought that once you knew the pathway of victory (faith in Christ and Him crucified), you would walk in constant victory. With my new knowledge, even though it was the truth, I was still missing something. What was I missing?

Then the Lord showed me how important it is that the believer renew his faith daily. I needed to keep my faith strong in what I knew to be true. If my faith weakened or if I took my eyes off Christ and the Cross for one day, I would begin to fail God again.

IT'S ALL ABOUT FAITH

"So then faith cometh by hearing, and hearing by the word of God" (Romans 10:17). And Jesus said if you want to follow Him, you have to *"pick up your cross daily"* (Luke 9:23)! Now the word *"daily"* hit me like a ton of bricks. I started to realize that each day in this life has its own challenges, and that I needed to approach every day of my life with the thought, *"I have to renew my faith today and walk in the power of the Spirit."* I knew that every new day I had to die to self all over again. The Apostle Paul said, *"I die daily"* (I Corinthians 15:31).

You see, every day is a challenge to live the victorious Christian life. The devil is not going to stop trying to get your eyes off Christ and Him crucified. You have to renew your faith in Christ and the Cross every day.

I had the revelation of the Cross, but I had to keep my faith strong in what I knew. I did this by reading, studying, and hearing the Word of God preached and taught. I had to spend time with Jesus daily. Each day I have to appropriate (take possession of) my faith in the Gospel of Jesus Christ. As I would do this, my faith would continue to grow and stay strong.

I have discovered that when my faith remains strong in the Cross of Calvary, the Holy Spirit continues to give me victory. And the way to keep your faith strong is to spend time every day in God's Word, in prayer, and continuously delighting yourself in Christ.

Once you learn the important truths about how to live, then you will begin to experience a wonderful freedom in the Lord. I am not perfect by any means—I still sin—but I have noticed that I sin less and less, Glory to God! God is perfecting my faith. It has changed me, and it is changing me (Philippians 1:6).

If your faith is in the right object, which is Christ and Him crucified, then you will definitely experience a revived relationship with the Lord. And, it just keeps getting better and better! You will go from victory to victory. All the praise goes to Jesus Christ and the Cross. For I will glory in nothing else but the Cross (Galatians 6:14)!

I will repeat what one preacher once said—I have never forgotten it: *"Don't ever separate Jesus and the Cross. When you think of Jesus, you should think of the Cross, and when you think of the Cross, you should think of Jesus."* Glory to God!

Chapter Two

Sin ... How It Entered The World

Why is there so much pain and suffering in the world? Why are little babies ripped from their mothers' wombs and never given a chance to live? Why would the government of the wealthiest and most prosperous nation in the world legalize such an act? Why are there so many incurable diseases that take the lives of millions each year? Why is there so much starvation in the world when there is enough food to feed all? Why do men take the lives of others? Why is there war? Why is there divorce, sexual immorality, rape, lying, stealing, fraud, physical abuse, profanity, anger, hatred, jealousy, envy? The list goes on and on.

There is only one answer to it all, and it's called sin. Sin has caused more pain, more heartache, more devastation and destruction than the human mind could ever imagine. Where did it all begin, and why did it have to happen? Could it have been avoided?

The word "sin" in the Greek is *"hamartia,"* which means *"missing the true goal and scope of life."* Man has missed the mark and fallen from the perfect state in which God created him. Romans 3:23 says, *"For all have sinned, and come short of the glory of God."* The glory of God is His splendor; and when a person commits a sin, at that moment he has fallen short of the glory or splendor of God. Because God is the righteous judge of His creation, He is left with only one verdict—guilty!

Mankind's sinfulness is an offense toward God, for sin is rebellion against God and His ways. Sin brings about death—spiritual death, which is separation from God.

Scientists do not know why the human body ages, because it is designed to rejuvenate itself about every seven years. Yet the Bible tells us why the human body ages and eventually dies—sin. The whole human race has been infected with this terrible disease,

17

for it is an inescapable truth that we will eventually die. The Bible declares, *"The wages of sin is death"* (Romans 6:23). The punishment for sin is spiritual death, which is eternal separation from a holy and perfect God.

Man, in his sinful state, has no real understanding of how horrible the act of sin is. Sin is a bold, outright denial of God's commands. Sin is saying, *"I'm going to do things my way, regardless of the consequences."* Ultimately, sin is saying to God, *"I am god, and my way is better than Your way."* This utter disrespect for a holy God and His perfect way leads to condemnation, judgment, and separation from God.

WHERE IT ALL BEGAN

The first sin was committed in the Garden of Eden, which many Bible scholars believe was located east of Israel, at the joining of the Tigris and Euphrates Rivers. Once the site of ancient Babylon, today it is known as Iraq.

The Bible says there came a day when Adam and Eve were walking in the Garden. The devil came to them as a serpent and began to speak to them. We know that the devil has the ability to disguise his real identity; the Bible says there are times the devil even disguises himself as an *"angel of light"* (II Corinthians 11:14).

Many people who read Genesis chapter 3 perhaps do not really understand the depth of what happened that day in the Garden of Eden. The pain, the heartache, and the suffering that resulted from Adam's and Eve's sin are unimaginable. However, Satan's way of deception—his pathway of destruction—is clearly laid out in these passages.

The devil took Eve on a downward slide that led her and Adam into committing the first sin, which in turn infected the whole of humanity. Let's look at exactly how this happened.

1. Satan first questioned God's Word and tried to twist it, wrongly stating what God really had said.

Now the serpent was more subtil than any beast of the field which the Lord God had made. And he said unto the woman, Yea, hath God said, Ye shall not eat of every tree of the garden?

Genesis 3:1

Satan is well aware that this is not what God said to Adam and Eve. Eve responded quickly to correct the serpent and said,

We may eat of the fruit of the trees of the garden: But of the fruit of the tree which is in the midst of the garden, God hath said, Ye shall not eat of it, neither shall ye touch it, lest ye die.

Genesis 3:2-3

Eve stated correctly what God had said—almost. In truth, God never told them they were not allowed to touch the fruit—she added that one. At least, it is not recorded in Scripture that God had said it. Remember, up to this point Adam and Eve have never disobeyed what God told them to do, and it had never even entered their minds to rebel against God's Word. But Satan cast his web of destruction carefully and subtly.

2. Satan went against what God had said; he lied to Eve. In essence, he called God a liar.

Genesis 3:4 says,

*And the serpent said unto the woman, Ye shall not surely die:"
Satan loves to lie to us and tries to persuade us that the consequences of sin are not that severe.*

All too often we make light of sin. We really don't concern ourselves with the judgment of sin, thinking, *"God wouldn't send a nice guy like me to hell."* The devil deceives us into thinking that sin is not that bad and we won't really die and spend eternity in hell for our sins. With the devil's help, we convince ourselves God does not really mean *"the wages of sin is death".*

These are lies from the devil, and mankind has believed them— that is why we see a lighthearted attitude over sinful behavior today.

Cross-Eyed

It is why people take sexual immorality, drunkenness, hatred, lying, stealing, gambling—you name it—lightly and consider these sins as normal living. Most people today don't see sin as a big deal—if they admit it exists at all. They have talked themselves into thinking God really doesn't mean what He says in the Bible about sin.

3. Satan presented the thought to Adam and Eve that God was misleading them and trying to keep them from being all they could be.

He presented them with the ultimate temptation—you can be a god! Genesis 3:5 says,

For God doth know that in the day ye eat thereof, then your eyes shall be opened, and ye shall be as gods, knowing good and evil.

In this verse we see the sinful desire of Satan that got him kicked out of heaven. The Bible teaches that originally Satan was an angel named Lucifer. He was one of the most beautiful angels God had ever created. There is also some evidence that he was gifted musically like no other. But due to pride, Lucifer wanted to be equal with his Creator and he rebelled, and therefore was thrown out of heaven and thrown down to the earth.

ADAM AND EVE WERE FOOLED

Adam and Eve bought the lie, and they ate from the tree. Genesis 3:6 says,

And when the woman saw that the tree was good for food, and that it was pleasant to the eyes, and a tree to be desired to make one wise, she took of the fruit thereof, and did eat, and gave also unto her husband with her; and he did eat.

Notice the progression of the original sin:

1. The Look— *"And when the woman saw that the tree was good...."* The tree looked good to Eve. Sin decorates itself to look good and tempts us. If it didn't look good, we wouldn't be tempted by it. So Satan dresses it up to look good. *"It was pleasant to the eyes."* Food is one of man's greatest needs, so Satan used it to deceive Adam and Eve.

20

SIN ... HOW IT ENTERED THE WORLD

2. The Thought—*"...and a tree to be desired to make one wise...."* The thought in Eve's mind was that by eating the fruit, it would benefit or help improve her position. Satan had deceived her thinking.

3. The Act—*"...she took of the fruit thereof and did eat..."* Eve disobeyed God's Word and sinned.

4. The Influence —*"and gave also unto her husband with her; and he did eat."* Eve gave the fruit to Adam and influenced his thinking toward sin as well.

Someone once said that man's greatest weakness is his inability to resist the persuasion of a woman. Satan usurped the authority of Adam by going to his wife first, but he used this to strike both of them.

Eve's taking the fruit and eating it was the second worst moment in human history. The worst moment in human history was when Adam ate the fruit—not when Eve ate it. Why? You would think that because Eve ate first, that was the worst moment. As terrible as it was, it was not worse than Adam eating the fruit. When Eve ate the fruit, sin entered the world; but it wasn't until Adam ate the fruit that sin could be passed onto the whole human race. The Bible declares that sin or the sin nature passes on from the seed of man, not from the woman. First Corinthians 15:22 says, *"For as in Adam all die."*

THE NATURE OF MAN

Sin could have begun and ended with Eve if Adam had refused to eat the fruit. But when Adam followed his wife's act of disobedience, he then became the chief carrier of the disease known as sin. Adam infected the whole human race. His seed, his very DNA, carried in it the sin nature, and he passed it from generation to generation. That is why King David used these words to describe the infectiousness of sin, *"Behold, I was shapen in iniquity; and in sin did my mother conceive me"* (Psalm 51:5).

When God created Adam and Eve, He gave them a *"human nature"* and a *"divine nature."* They had a human conscience, and

21

they had a God consciousness. When they sinned, they lost their God consciousness. It was replaced with a *"sin nature."*

After they sinned by eating the fruit (which we refer to as the Fall of Man), they recognized they were naked and they were ashamed. *"And the eyes of them both were opened, and they knew that they were naked; and they sewed fig leaves together, and made themselves aprons"* (Genesis 3:7). The veil of innocence fell from their eyes. They lost God consciousness and gained sin consciousness or a sin nature.

Every person on the face of the earth has at least two natures: our human nature (the ability to feel love, joy, pain, and suffering), and our sin nature (our ability or desire to rebel against God).

Jesus was born without a sin nature because He was not conceived by man but was conceived by the Holy Spirit. Therefore He was born without sin. But he was tempted, and had He given into temptation as did Adam and Eve, He would have fallen and received a sin nature just as Adam and Eve did.

Whenever a person comes to Christ and is born of the Spirit, he then is given a third nature. At the moment of salvation, we receive a divine nature. Second Peter 1:4 says,

> *Whereby are given unto us exceeding great and precious promises: that by these ye might be partakers of the <u>divine nature</u>, having escaped the corruption that is in the world through lust. (emphasis added)*

The Holy Spirit [the divine nature] enters when we invite Christ into our lives. The divine nature cannot sin, for it is holy and hates sin. This divine nature wars against the sin nature (the flesh) in our lives. Galatians 5:17 says,

> *For the flesh lusteth against the Spirit, and the Spirit against the flesh: and these are contrary the one to the other: so that ye cannot do the things that ye would.*

The sin nature has redefined what is right and what is wrong. This is the problem that has plagued the world since Adam's day in the Garden.

Could It Have Been Avoided?

Could humanity have avoided falling into sin? Yes! But man chose to go his own separate way. One could say, *"Well, God knew that man would disobey Him and that sin would enter the world, and He knew the destruction that would follow. So why did He still create man, and why did He give us the ability to make wrong choices?"* We don't know the answer to that question, but we do know that God loves His creation (John 3:16). He has also provided a way for man to come back to Him and a way to stop the destruction—the way of the Cross (John 14:6).

Man today cannot change the original sin or the fact that we are conceived with a sin nature. However, man is accountable for accepting or rejecting the solution to the sin nature, which is what Christ did on the Cross to save us from our sin.

Understanding The Seriousness Of Sin

Most people do not understand the wretchedness of their sins and how they have caused separation from God. I constantly hear people who seem to assume that a *"good"* life should be enough, as though good works are enough to outweigh the cost of our sins. Some preachers are now saying that any legitimate search for God—whether it be by a Hindu, a Muslim, or a person of some other religion—is enough and that Jesus died for everyone, whether they accept Him or not.

Despite their wishful thinking, this is not what the Bible teaches. Good works are not enough to save us, and not everyone will go to heaven (Ephesians 2:8-9, John 3:16-18). The Word is very clear that we must believe in Jesus Christ as our Lord and Savior, acknowledge what He did on the Cross to save us, and repent of our sins. People who fall short of this will not enter God's Kingdom and be with Him for eternity.

Sin is serious business to God and it has serious consequences— death for eternity. We have an important decision to make. God does not want any of us to spend eternity separated from Him. Second Peter 3:9 says, *"The Lord is not slack concerning His promise, as some men count slackness; but is longsuffering to us-ward, not willing that any should perish, but that all should come to repentance."* He does not desire any of His little ones to perish (Matthew 18:14).

God has given every person a choice and a free will to choose or reject Him. The Bible says,

> *I call heaven and earth to record this day against you, that I have set before you life and death, blessing and cursing: therefore choose life, that both thou and thy seed may live.*

Deuteronomy 30:19

Chapter Three

The Sin Nature Versus The Divine Nature

In understanding the problem of sin, we must go to the root, which is the sin nature. This is the evil nature that lives within every human being, and it is a nature that rebels against God's laws. When we were conceived, we were given a human nature and a sin nature. That is why we don't have to teach children to lie, but we have to teach them to tell the truth. We don't have to teach children to be selfish, that comes naturally, but we do have to teach them how to share.

When a person comes to faith in Christ, the sin nature is dethroned (detached) from controlling that person's life. In Romans chapter 6, Paul explains how a believer is saved and how the Holy Spirit defeats the sin nature. Romans 6 is one of the most important chapters in the Bible, for without properly understanding it, the believer will live in defeat.

ROMANS SIX

Paul begins to explain the mechanics of how the Spirit brings about victory over sin. If we are going to live the victorious Christian life, we must understand how the Holy Spirit functions within our lives.

Paul makes it clear that if a person is truly saved, it is impossible to live a life of habitual sin. He shows that the Christian has changed masters and that the new nature (divine nature) he has received from the Lord is not a nature of sin, but a nature that is completely righteous. Romans 6:22 says, *"But now being made free from sin, and become servants to God, ye have your fruit unto holiness, and the end everlasting life."*

Paul uses the definite article *"the"* before the word *"sin"* in most of the references in Romans 6. So when Paul uses the word *"sin,"* he is not merely speaking of the act of sin but he is speaking of

25

the sin nature. Every time we see the word *"sin,"* substitute *"sinful nature"* (except in verse 15 where he is referring to the act of sin) and see the flood of light that is thrown upon our understanding.[1]

As we have already stated, we are born with both a human nature and a sin nature (Psalm 51:5 and Romans 3:23). Before we are saved, our lives are ruled by our sin nature—we sin habitually, and we don't really think anything of it. But when we become born again, we are given a divine nature through the Holy Spirit, who comes to abide within our hearts and lives.

Now that we are partakers of the divine nature, should we continue to sin? Paul asked this question in Romans 6:1, when he said (paraphrase), *"Should we continue to allow the sin nature to rule and dominate our life so that grace will abound?"* His answer to that question is, *"God forbid!"*

To have victory over the sin nature, the first thing we must know is that our sin nature is not eradicated (removed) when we are saved; it is simply dethroned, defused, made ineffective.

Different Views On The Sin Nature

Let's look at the different views that believers typically take when dealing with the Sin Nature:

1. Denial—Once he is saved, the believer does not believe that he has a sin nature.

2. Ignorance—The believer does not study the Bible and therefore is ignorant of what the Bible says regarding the sin nature. If not dealt with, this lack of knowledge will leave the believer completely defeated. Even worse, if not dealt with, the sin nature can cause him to leave the faith altogether.

3. License—The person believes that because he has been saved by grace, he can sin willfully and grace will cover his sins.

4. Struggle—Most believers struggle with the sin nature, and the harder they try to control it, the more they sin. They are living the defeated Christian life.

5. Grace—The person understands grace and how the Holy Spirit works through our faith in Christ and Him crucified. He is living the abundant life that Jesus promised for every believer (John 10:10).

If the believer ignores what Paul taught in Romans 6, he is in essence rejecting the prescribed order of victory over sin, which will result in all kinds of bondage. Without properly understanding Romans 6, the believer will experience a Christian life filled with a cycle of sinning and repenting—defeat!

Romans 6:14 uses the word *"dominion."* The Greek word for *"dominion"* is *"kurieuo,"* and it means *"to be lord of"* or *"to exercise lordship over."* Before we were saved, sin was our lord. It was our master, we bowed to it every day; it dominated our lives. But once we came to Christ, we went from living under the law to living under grace. At the moment of salvation, the Lord through His Holy Spirit dethroned our old master, the sin nature, and placed Christ on the throne of our lives.

Romans 6:7 says, *"For he that is dead is freed from sin [the sin nature]."* Another translation puts it, *"For when we died with Christ we were set free from the power of sin"* (NLT). Every believer must know this verse!

The sin nature does not die when we get saved; but we must now die to the sin nature daily. This is an act of will and an act of faith by the believer. Christians are to be dead to sin! Physical death separates a person's soul from his body. Spiritual death separates the person from God. When a believer comes to Christ, he dies to (is separated from) his sin nature! God uses His divine scalpel to cut the believer loose from his sin nature. The Holy Spirit circumcises [cuts away] the sin nature from controlling our lives, and He places the divine nature on the throne of our heart (Colossians 2:11-15).

When we get saved, we don't live a sinless life or a life of moral perfection. This is evidence that the sin nature is not taken away from believers. The Bible makes this clear in I John 1:8: *"If we say that we have no sin, we deceive ourselves, and the truth is not in us."*

But at your moment of salvation, God dethrones the sin nature as the lord of your life. How does He do this? Upon your faith in Jesus Christ and what He did on the Cross, God identifies you with the death, burial, and resurrection of Christ. He will begin to change the way you walk, and the way you talk. Your desires will begin to change. Your goals will change. The way you view the world will change. God will change your priorities, and chief among these new priorities will be your love for other people's eternal destination. These are all effects of the divine nature being placed within your heart and life.

THE DOUBLE CURE OF THE CROSS

In Romans 6:3, scripture says, *"Know ye not, that so many of us as were baptized into Jesus Christ were baptized into his death?"* This verse is not speaking of water baptism (as some teach), but it is dealing with a spiritual immersion that takes place at the moment we each come to faith in Jesus Christ. When we place our faith in Christ, we are identified with Him in His death on the Cross.

The death of our Lord had a two-fold impact on sin. He died for our acts of sin (Romans 3:21-5:11), and He died for our sinful nature. His death brings separation between the believer and the sin nature.

Read the words of the song *"Rock of Ages"*:

*"Let the water and the blood,
from thy riven side which flowed,
be of sin the double cure,
save from wrath and make me pure."*

"Saved from wrath" is what we call justification; and *"make me pure"* is sanctification, the breaking of the power of the indwelling sin nature. Our Lord's death not only paid the penalty of human sin, it also broke the power of the indwelling sin nature in our lives. That is the double cure! Where did that happen? At the Cross!

The Greek word for *"baptized"* is *"baptizo"*, and it means *"to immerse or submerge."* It is the *"introduction or placing of a person or things into a new environment or into union with something else so as to alter its condition or relationship to its previous environment or condition."* [2]

28

The believing sinner, upon proper faith in Christ and Him crucified, is baptized into Jesus Christ's death, burial, and resurrection (Romans 6:2-4). The believing sinner, by an act of God, enters into a vital union with Jesus Christ, whereby his sin nature is separated from his inner being, and he is totally identified with Christ. He is placed into a new existence, free from a life of sin, to know a life of pleasing God.

All of this is performed by repentance and simple faith in Christ. We are not saved by what we do, we are saved by what we believe. In Romans 6, when explaining how one is saved, Paul uses the term *"know"* six times between Romans 6:1 and Romans 7:1. Circle the word *"know"* or *"knowing"* in your Bibles as a reminder.

SO WHAT DO YOU KNOW?

The Bible stresses *"knowing"* because the whole Christian faith operates through faith in what Jesus did at Calvary. Romans 6:6 says we know this: *"...that our old man is crucified with him, that the body of sin might be destroyed, that henceforth we should not serve sin."*

"The old man" in this verse is the person we were before we got saved. This word *"old"* in the Greek means *"to be worn out, useless, fit to be put on the scrap pile, to be discarded."* That is a very graphic description, but that is who we were before becoming Christians. An unsaved person is depraved, unregenerate, lacking the life of God.

The phrase *"body of sin"* is speaking of the physical body being possessed, controlled, or dominated by the sin nature. The word *"destroyed"* in the Greek is *"katargeo,"* and it means *"to render idle, inactive, inoperative and means to make void, or ineffective."* It does not refer to annihilation, as some teach! While the sin nature is not removed at conversion, it is made ineffective.

This is all made possible by what Christ did on the Cross. When the Lord saves, He defuses the sin nature's power over the individual; He takes the sin nature and renders it idle, ineffective or inactive. But the Lord does not take away the Christian's free will and does not treat him as a machine. So it is possible for the believer to reconnect himself with the sin nature by his own choosing, bringing sin back into his life.

Now That I Am Saved

We now know that our old man (that is, our worn-out, sinful man) was killed with Christ at the Cross (by faith), and the new nature (the divine nature) was implanted in our hearts due to the resurrection of Christ. Romans 6:4 says, *"Therefore we are buried with him by baptism into death: that as Christ was raised up from the dead by the glory of the Father, even so we also should walk in newness of life."* Notice the resurrection of Jesus has now given us a new life. We should walk in that new life as believers in Christ.

If the new believer does not understand this inner change and adjust himself to it properly, he or she will live a mediocre Christian life. The inner spiritual machinery installed by the Holy Spirit at the moment of salvation needs to be serviced regularly. There are two things the believer must do to expect the best results in this new world called the Christian life.

The first thing is reckon (consider) yourself dead to the sin nature. Romans 6:11 says, *"Likewise reckon ye also yourselves to be dead indeed unto sin, but alive unto God through Jesus Christ our Lord."*

The word *"reckon"* is an accounting term. The Greek word is *"logizomai,"* which means *"to count, compute, to take into account."* The believer, by faith, must compute in his mind every day, all the time, the biblical fact that he is dead to the sin nature. It no longer has control over him because of what Christ did at the Cross. The believer is now alive to God through Jesus Christ. Jesus broke the grip of the sin nature at the Cross for every believer, and God gave him the divine nature through the person of the Holy Spirit.

The believer who has placed his faith in Christ, and has *"reckoned"* himself dead to sin should no longer struggle with the things that he struggled with before coming to Christ. When you as a believer are struggling with sin, get in the Word and begin to exercise your faith and belief in the finished work of the Cross. Satan and his powers cannot stand up to the blood of Christ. It drives him crazy because He can't compete with it—it's too powerful!

Secondly, the believer must yield to the working of the Holy Spirit. God will not override your will. So there must be a daily submitting or yielding to the workings of the Holy Spirit. Romans 6:13 says, *"Neither yield ye your members as instruments of unrighteousness unto sin: but yield yourselves unto God, as those that are alive from the dead, and your members as instruments of righteousness unto God."* The believer still must *"yield"* his will to God every day if he is going to reap the benefits of the Cross.

Now, what does the Bible mean when it says *"yield your members"*? Your members are your body, your sense of touch, smell, sight, hearing, and taste. Paul is saying to yield these members unto God. The Greek word for *"yield"* is *"paristemi,"* and it means *"to present, to give way, bring before, etc."*

When the believer yields his members to the Holy Spirit, he in essence is coming before God and not leaning on his own ability to resist sin. He is leaning on the assistance of the Holy Spirit to live the Christian life through him. This is what it means to have total dependence on God and not on self. Jesus said it clearly in John 15:5, *"I am the vine, ye are the branches: He that abideth in me, and I in him, the same bringeth forth much fruit: for without me ye can do nothing."*

Jesus is saying He is the vine to the branch. He is the lifeline to us. To get the life or spiritual energy to live the Christian life, we have to abide in Him. Abiding in Christ is the key to it all. The word *"abide"* in the Greek is *"meno"* which means *"to stay in a given place, state, or relation."* It means to continue or remain in the same relationship with Christ that we were in at the moment of salvation.

Think about it for a moment; where was the Holy Spirit five seconds before you got saved? Was He outside of you or inside of you? He was outside of you convicting you of sin. What was it that caused the Holy Spirit to perform the greatest miracle known to man, spiritual regeneration? It was faith in what Christ did at the Cross for you.

When a person gets saved, he humbles himself and admits he is a sinner and needs a Savior. He repents (turns) from his sins.

Cross-Eyed

This is a changing of mind regarding sinful living, and he turns toward God. He places faith in Christ and Him crucified, and God responds by sending the Holy Spirit into that individual's life. He performs the greatest miracle ever known to man—the miracle of new birth.

At the moment of salvation, you learn what moves the Holy Spirit. It is faith in Christ and Him crucified alone that gives you victory. Now stay there! Don't move your faith from that simple truth of the Gospel.

THE BELIEVER CHANGES MASTERS

Romans 6:16 says,

Know ye not, that to whom ye yield yourselves servants to obey, his servants ye are to whom ye obey; whether of sin unto death, or of obedience unto righteousness?

The Christian changes masters. Before Christ, we were servants of sin and the devil. Jesus said, *"Ye are of your father the devil"* (John 8:44). Now we are servants of the Lord. We change masters because we are given new natures that want to serve God and run from evil. The true believer hates sin and endeavors to keep sin out of his life.

The word *"servants"* in the Greek is *"doulos,"* which means *"a slave of another."* It also means *"one who serves another to the disregard of his own interests."* When living in an unsaved state, we were living for sin, and we were serving the devil with a disregard for God or our own best interests. We were sinners, and we were experiencing death (separation from God), sorrow, and suffering.

But now the believer, of his own will, serves the Lord Jesus with an abandon that says, *"Nothing matters about me, just so long as the Lord Jesus is glorified."*[3]

God's grace is free, that's why it's called grace; and He gives His grace to sinners, that's why it's called *"Amazing."*

Chapter Four

How is The Sinner Saved?

The Bible defines sin as *"knowing what the right thing is to do and not doing it"* (James 4:17). When a person rebels against God's law, he becomes a transgressor of the law and therefore, in the eyes of God, he is a sinner.

There is a penalty for man's sin, and that penalty is eternal damnation. There is a saying in life *"you get what you paid for."* If a person lives a life of sin, which is rebelling against God and His laws, then on Judgment Day that person will get what he paid for, eternal death in a place called hell.

Revelation 20:12-13 says,

> *And I saw the dead, small and great, stand before God; and the books were opened: and another book was opened, which is the book of life: and the dead were judged out of those things which were written in the books, according to their works. And the sea gave up the dead which were in it; and death and hell delivered up the dead which were in them: and they were judged every man according to their works.*

We all know about the first death, which is when a person takes his final breath and slips into eternity. However, we don't hear much about the second death. The second death occurs after a person faces the Great White Throne Judgment, when God Almighty judges the world for its sins Revelation 20:11-15.

WHAT IS THE LAKE OF FIRE?

The Lake of Fire is the place where the sinner who has rebelled against God will spend all eternity. When studying about hell, one needs to look no farther than the words of Jesus Christ because Jesus spoke more about hell then anyone else in the Bible. Why? Jesus came to this earth to give us a way to avoid going to hell.

Cross-Eyed

In speaking about hell, Jesus gave us the following truths about this horrible place:

- It is a place of torment (Luke 16:23).

- There is a consciousness in hell, and family and friends are remembered (Luke 16:23-31).

- There is a lack of water (Luke 16:24).

- There are flames of fire burning perpetually (Luke 16:24, Mark 9:47-48).

- The person in hell wants to escape, but cannot (Luke 16:26).

- He wishes he had repented while on earth, but now it is too late (Luke 16:30). Each person lives in eternal regret and misery for rejecting Christ as his Savior.

- There is gnashing of teeth (Matthew 13:50). Great fear and remorse are there.

- Crying, weeping and wailing are in hell (Matthew 8:12, 13:42).

- There is outer darkness in hell (Matthew 8:12).

- Hell is forever and forever (Matthew 25:46). It is eternal!

God never created hell for people, but He created it for Satan and all the demons. Jesus said, *"Then shall He say also unto them on the left hand, depart from me, ye cursed, into everlasting fire, prepared for the devil and his angels"* (Matthew 25:41). Hell was prepared by God for the devil and all the fallen angels who joined in Lucifer's revolution. The Bible teaches us that Lucifer was a beautiful angel created by God who became enamored with his own beauty (pride) and wanted to be exalted above God. He led a rebellion in heaven against God, and one third of the angels joined with him. They all fell from heaven and became what we know today as *"demons"* or in essence *"fallen angels"* (Ezekiel 28:14-19, Luke 10:18).

The Bible is clear: God does not want any person to spend eternity in hell. Look at the words of II Peter 3:9,

34

The Lord is not slack concerning his promise, as some men count slackness; but is longsuffering to us-ward, not willing that any should perish, but that all should come to repentance.

The key words in the above verse are *"any"* and *"all"*. God does not want *"any"* of His creation to spend eternity in hell. He wants *"all"* to be saved. That is why He sent His one and only Son to die on the Cross so that the world could be saved. For God so loved the world that He gave His only Son to die for all sinners (John 3:16). But men and women send themselves to hell by their own rejection of God's only solution for sin, Jesus Christ and Him crucified (I Corinthians 1:18).

Consider the consequences of living this life in sin: spending forever in a place of fire, weeping, with unquenchable thirst, and loneliness. Compare that against the reward of living this life for God: living eternally in peace, health, joy and extreme beauty in a place God calls paradise. The choice would seem like a *"no brainer."* But the devil has done a good job of turning the heart of man against God and His ways.

Amazing Grace

If there is a Christian theme song, I guess it would be the song Amazing Grace. The words of the song are profound and have been sung by countless millions.

"Amazing Grace, how sweet the sound that saved a wretch like me. I once was lost, but now I'm found. I was blind, but now I see."

The word *"Grace"* means *"unmerited or undeserved favor."* Man's religion tells us that we have to earn God's favor, but the Bible teaches that grace cannot be earned, it can only be received as a free gift. I think the concept of earning your way to heaven has sent more people to hell then anything else in life. All along the Bible has taught us that God's favor cannot be earned; it is only through God's amazing grace that we can be saved.

The great Apostle Paul, who wrote nearly one-third of the New Testament and was arguably the most anointed and most-used man of God in the Bible, made this confession of himself:

> *"For I know that in me (that is, in my flesh,) dwelleth no good thing: for to will is present with me; but how to perform that which is good I find not".*

Romans 7:18

Now let's stop for a moment and think. If the Apostle Paul believed that there wasn't any good thing in him apart from God and he couldn't live a righteous life without the power of the Holy Spirit, then how have so many come to believe that by just *"being a good person"* they can make it into heaven. That is a lie from the devil, and millions have bought it.

The only thing that makes a man righteous (good) is when he places his faith in Jesus Christ and what Jesus did for him at the Cross, and he invites Jesus to come into his life to save him. When the Spirit (the Spirit of Christ) comes into a person's heart, then God can declare that person righteous because He sees His perfect Son inside him. This eliminates all boasting by the person. The Bible says in Ephesians 2:8-9,

> *For by grace are you saved through faith; and that not of yourselves: it is the gift of God: Not of works, lest any man should boast.*

Many times after a person comes to Jesus and experiences the new birth (John 3:3), he begins to shift his faith back to himself and tries to be a good person by his own efforts. Defeat will surely follow, as he is not living for God in the right way. The Bible clearly teaches us that the same way you come to Christ (faith and repentance) is the same way you are now to live every day in relationship with Christ. *"As ye have therefore received Christ Jesus the Lord, so walk ye in him"* (Colossians 2:6).

Many believers think that they can live the Christian life by diligently keeping some form of Christian discipline. But this is a sure way to fail. We must continually walk before God with a repentant heart, dependent on the victory of the Cross and the power of the Holy Spirit so we can live a victorious life free from sin and the bondages of sin.

Daily faith and daily repentance must be present in the Christian's life in order to live in victory. Without faith, repentance becomes only despair; and without repentance, faith is only presumption (Swaggart). Having one without the other will only result in a *"false conversion."* But when the two are joined together, redemption in Christ is found. Acts 20:21 says,

> *Testifying both to the Jews, and also to the Greeks, repentance toward God, and faith toward our Lord Jesus Christ.*

Repentance

Repentance is one of the greatest gifts that God has ever given mankind; it is the way out of judgment.

The word *"repentance"* in the Greek is *"metanoeo"* and means to have *"regret over one's sins and a true change of heart toward God."* The repenting sinner wants to change the course of his life, and he understands that only God can do that.

There are people who are living strict moral lives that look pretty good on the outside. However, on the inside their hearts are wicked and filled with lust, greed, jealousy, envy, hatred, rebellion, etc. A person may fool others, but he can't fool God. We have all offended a holy and righteous God. Repentance is acknowledging that offense and wanting to turn from it.

People who truly repent will experience the conviction (guilt) of sin and the sorrow it has caused God. When King David committed the sin of adultery with Bathsheba, he made the remorseful confession,

> *Against thee, thee only, have I sinned, and done this evil in thy sight: that thou mightest be justified when thou speakest, and be clear when thou judgest.*

> Psalm 51:4

True repentance occurs when you acknowledge that you have sinned against God, that what you've done is evil, and you experience remorse in your heart for disobeying God. When you experience this, you desire to turn from selfish disobedience against God to a life of obeying Him. This can only happen when the Holy Spirit is moving upon a person's heart and life.

Believe In The Gospel

In Mark 1:15, Jesus said *"believe in the Gospel." "believe"* and *"faith"* are interchangeable words when used in the Bible. The Greek word *"believe"* is *"pisteuo"* and means a *"mental persuasion and opinion, a confidence in."*

The word *"faith"* means to *"believe in or to put total trust in."* The Greek word for faith is *"pistis"*, which means *"to persuade,"* producing good works. Faith is the second condition given by Jesus for Salvation.

It is not faith in faith that will save a person; but it is the object of faith that is the key. If you are trusting in your good works to save you or if your faith is in God being a good God and He will let you slide on sin when you stand before Him at the Judgment Seat, then you are in deep trouble. If you are trusting in your priest, pastor, your church denomination or some religious act such as communion or water baptism to save you, then your faith is misplaced and you will be judged for your sins.

The proper object of faith is Jesus Christ and Him crucified. Jesus is the Son of God, Emmanuel, God in the flesh. What Jesus did on the Cross to pay for the penalty of our sins (Galatians 2:20-21) is the right object of faith. The Bible calls God's salvation plan the *"Gospel,"* and to be saved, we must believe in it.

> *Moreover, brethren, I declare unto you the gospel which I preached unto you, which also ye have received, and wherein ye stand; By which also ye are saved, if ye keep in memory what I preached unto you, unless ye have believed in vain.*

> *For I delivered unto you first of all that which I also received, how that Christ died for our sins according to the scriptures; And that he was buried, and that he rose again the third day according to the scriptures.*

> I Corinthians 15:1-4

The word *"Gospel"* in the Greek is *"euaggellon,"* which means the *"good news."* The Gospel is the basic facts of the death, burial, and resurrection of Jesus Christ, and the interpretation of these facts. The good news of the kingdom of God is that there is salvation through Jesus Christ.

Believing in the Gospel means that you are totally assured of the death, burial, and resurrection of Jesus Christ as the means by which Salvation is received. This does not mean a mere intellectual belief, but a complete trust with all your heart that Christ specifically died for you to become your Savior when you ask Him into your heart.

You trust exclusively in what Christ did for you on the Cross to save you from the penalty and power of sin. That is what makes the good news, the good news! You believe that what Jesus did on the Cross was personally for you.

The Gospel of Christ reveals to us that Jesus is the source of Salvation, and the Cross is the means of Salvation. Only the shed blood of Jesus can deliver the sinner from eternal Judgment. God the Father did not accept anything other than the perfect sacrifice of His Son's death on the Cross. The Apostle Paul knew that the true object of his faith was Jesus Christ (who He is) and Him crucified (what He did). The Bible doesn't teach that we can get to heaven by being a good person or by doing good works. If we could get to heaven by being good, then why would God send His Son to suffer and die?

The Bible clearly teaches that salvation is through faith (belief) in the Son of God who loves you and died for you. Galatians 2:20 says,

> *I am crucified with Christ: nevertheless I live; yet not I, but Christ liveth in me: and the life which I now live in the flesh I live by the faith of the Son of God, who loved me, and gave himself for me.*

When you become a Christian, there is a change in your life. The above verse says *"the life that I now live."* Before putting your faith in Christ, you are living a life without Christ. But when you put your faith in the Son of God and what He did at the Cross, then Christ comes in and lives inside of you. This is the miracle of the new birth (John 3:3).

BIBLE NAMES

God could have called His Son any name He wanted, but He chose to call the second person of the Trinity *"Jesus Christ."* The name *"Jesus Christ"* is a prophetic look at who Jesus is and what His mission was. The name *"Jesus"* means *"Savior,"* which pertains to His mission (what He came to do). It has to do with the Cross and His death on that Cross for the sins of the world. When one thinks of Jesus, one should think of the Cross. When one thinks of the Cross, one should think of Jesus. We should never separate Jesus from the Cross. Although Jesus was a great prophet, teacher, healer, and more, His main mission was to be a Savior and to die on the Cross for the sins of the world.

The name *"Christ"* means *"Messiah"* or *"Anointed One."* This speaks of who Jesus is. He was and is the Messiah, the one sent by God to save His people from their sins.

Christianity is all about Jesus Christ, who He is, and what He did. When one believes by faith in Christ as Messiah and Savior and repents (turns) from sin, turning his life over to Jesus, then and only then can one be born again and saved from an eternal hell. It is the most important decision one will ever make in his lifetime.

JUSTIFICATION BY FAITH

The word *"justification"* is a legal term and the Greek word for it is *"dikaloo,"* which means *"to make righteous,"* or to declare one as not guilty. Some have explained justification as meaning *"just as if I never sinned."* In the eyes of God, when you repent of your sins, put your faith in Christ and what Christ did at the Cross for you, and receive Him into your heart and life, God then no longer sees your sinful heart but sees the righteousness of His holy Son abiding there. That is why the New Testament scriptures use the term over and over *"in Christ"* when referring to the believer. They don't say Jesus is in us, but they say that we are in Christ.

A believer in Christ needs to understand the phrase *"the just shall live by faith."* This phrase, found in Romans 1:17, presents the truth that faith in Christ and what He did through the Cross is what justifies us (declares the believer as *"not guilty"*). In Romans 5:1, the Apostle Paul says, *"Therefore being justified by faith, we have peace with God through our Lord Jesus Christ."*

The Bible doesn't teach that we are saved by our own works but that we are saved by the work of Christ on the Cross. That finished work cannot be improved upon, but only accepted. Sinful man is not saved by what he does or doesn't do; he is saved by what he believes. John 3:16 teaches *"whosoever believes in Him should not perish, but have everlasting life."*

All the other major religions of the world instruct people how to live within set rules and regulations. The followers of these belief systems are taught that if they submit to these rules and regulations, they can earn their way to heaven. Every religion except Christianity teaches justification by works.

These other religions are false paths to heaven and have no doubt led countless millions to eternal death-separation from God for eternity. The Bible teaches that all of man's attempts at righteous acts are filthy rags in the eyes of a perfect and righteous God (Isaiah 64:6).

God, the creator of man, tells us what is needed for us to be saved. There is nothing we can do in our own strength or willpower to make ourselves acceptable unto God. Remember what Paul said in Romans 7:18, *"For I know that in me (that is, in my flesh,) dwelleth no good thing."* Everything good (in the eyes of God) that dwells in me is the goodness of the Spirit. Jesus said in John 15:5, *"apart from Me, you can do nothing."* When will mankind understand the important truth that we desperately need God?

Every man and woman who has ever been born since Adam (except Christ) was born a sinner in need of a Savior. We all stand guilty on all accounts. Romans 3:23 says, *"For all have sinned and come short of the glory of God."*

Cross-Eyed

God sent His only begotten Son to earth to be our substitute on the Cross. Jesus took our punishment for sin. He hung on the Cross and suffered the judgment for our rebellion against God. Only the blood of Jesus can cleanse us and make us clean. The Apostle Paul, one of the men God used the most, referred to himself as the greatest of all sinners and the least of all saints. That is how we should all look at ourselves.

The only requirement to receive God's forgiveness is to have a heart that regrets the sins committed, that turns from a life of sin, and believes and trusts in what Jesus did at the Cross. Scripture says that we are justified freely by the grace of God through the redemption of what Jesus did at the Cross (Romans 3:24).

The first place that we learn about *"justification by faith"* in the Bible concerns a man in the Old Testament named Abraham. The Bible says that *"For what saith the scripture? Abraham believed God, and it was counted unto him for righteousness"* (Romans 4:3). Abraham did not earn God's favor, for he was an unrighteous man, but he received it by grace (unmerited or unearned favor) through faith. Jesus, when speaking of Abraham, said *"Abraham rejoiced to see my day, and he saw it, and was glad"* (John 8:56). You see, today we look back to the Cross and believe, but the Old Testament saints looked ahead to the Cross and believed.

GOD'S SPIRITUAL OPERATION

When someone has a diseased organ in his body, the medical surgeons go in and cut out the defective organ to cure the person. The Bible teaches that when we put our faith in Jesus Christ and Him crucified, then God performs a spiritual operation on us.

The Bible says in Colossians 2:11,

> *In whom also ye are circumcised with the circumcision made without hands, in putting off the body of the sins of the flesh by the circumcision of Christ.*

The word *"circumcision"* means *"to cut away"*. The Bible says that when we are born again, God spiritually circumcises our flesh; God through His Spirit cuts away the flesh (the sin nature). However, unlike the medical physician, He does not remove the sin nature from us, He simply cuts away its control over us. But if the new believer doesn't know how to walk with God in the Spirit (Galatians 5:16), then the sin nature can reattach itself to the person.

At the moment of Salvation, God not only cuts away the flesh (the sin nature), but He also deposits something into the new believer. He places His *"divine nature"* into the repenting sinner. The Bible says in II Peter 1:4,

> *Whereby are given unto us exceeding great and precious promises: that by these ye might be partakers of the divine nature, having escaped the corruption that is in the world through lust.*

At the moment that a person receives the *"divine nature"* (which is the Holy Spirit now dwelling in the believer's heart and life), the following miracles simultaneously happen as a result of the new birth.

- God baptizes (immerses) the individual or places the new believer into the Body of Christ (I Corinthians 12:13). Now the person is identified with Christ and belongs to the family of God. He has been adopted into a large family that is worldwide and stretches over many generations.

- He justifies the person, which means He declares him not guilty (Romans 5:1).

- He sanctifies the person, which means He makes him holy and set apart (Romans 15:16).

- He glorifies the person, in that He places that person's future in heaven, and the person is assured of a new glorified body that will live forever (Romans 8:30).

The Lord does much more than this at the moment of salvation, but these are the four main things He does through His Spirit. This spiritual operation by the Holy Spirit leaves a person totally changed. It is a miracle, and it is referred by Jesus as being *"born again"* (John 3:3).

Cross-Eyed

One of the very important aspects of the Holy Spirit's operation which we call the new birth is *"sanctification."* This means *"to be made holy."* If we believers do not understand how we are sanctified or how ongoing sanctification works, then we are going to run into all kinds of problems and will live the defeated Christian life.

SANCTIFICATION BY FAITH

Once a person is saved, his or her life takes on greater meaning and purpose. The new believer in Christ is now on a journey to move closer and closer to God. In James 4:8 the Bible says, *"Draw near to God and He will draw near to you."*

When translated from the Greek, this verse has greater light. It says, *"Draw nearer to God and He will draw nearer to you."* This means that the believer in Christ should always be on a lifelong pursuit of knowing God in a greater way.

The goal of the Christian life is not to be happy and blessed; that is simply a byproduct. The will of God for all believers in Christ is to be holy as He is holy – God commands us to be holy (Ephesians 1:4, I Peter 1:15-16). First Thessalonians 4:3 says, *"For this is the will of God, even your sanctification."*

Now the word *"sanctification"* in the Greek is *"hagiasmos,"* and it means to be holy or separated unto God. This word not only means the activity of the Holy Spirit to set man apart unto salvation, but also enabling him to be holy even as God is holy.

When you are saved, the Holy Spirit justifies you and prepares you for sanctification by cleansing you from sin. But now the Holy Spirit is present in your life to change your behavior and make you holy. The question is: How does the Holy Spirit do that?

First of all, you the believer in Christ must understand that the same faith that saved you is the same faith that sanctifies you. This is a huge truth that must be understood by every Christian. The tendency is to think that you have to work for holiness or somehow earn it. Just as your salvation cannot be earned or achieved by human effort, so is sanctification granted to the believer in the same way.

Many people in the Church lacking faith in the finished work of Christ on the Cross look to such things as Christian disciplines or human psychology to provide answers to their struggles against sin. Human psychology, although having some ability to analyze the problems, has no power to set the person free from the bondages of sin. Therefore the Church must not look to some secular means to lead people out of sin and corruption, but must look exclusively to the Cross.

Those in the Church who are pointing the addicted, afflicted and bruised to some twelve-step program or some professional counseling which is steeped in man's methods of setting man free are actually leading the blind astray. Jesus called it the blind leading the blind and the result will be exactly what Jesus said, *"both fall into the ditch"* (Matthew 15:14).

When we emphasize what we must *"do"* to be free from sin, rather than simply believing in what Christ did, we are not only heading in the wrong direction, but we are actually working against the solution. Human intellect, personal willpower, good works, or some new counseling technique will not set the sinners free and it will not break the strongholds of the enemy in the believers' lives. Only-and I emphasize only-faith in the blood of Christ sets us free.

The Bible says in Ephesians 1:7, *"In whom we have redemption through his blood, the forgiveness of sins, according to the riches of his grace."* The word *"redemption"* in the Greek is *"apolutrosis,"* and it means to release on payment of ransom. The blood of Jesus has paid the price for our release from sin and the corruption of sin. Only the blood can set us free. The devil will not loose his grip to anything else!

A FINISHED WORK

When Jesus hung on the Cross, His last words were, *"It is finished"* (John 19:30). Jesus' work on Calvary, the place where the Cross was hung, is a finished work, meaning nothing needs to be added. So when Christ said, *"it is finished,"* He was saying the work for man's freedom is done.

Cross-Eyed

When Jesus ascended to Heaven, He sat down at the right hand of the Father. In fact, every time except for one, when we see Jesus in Heaven, He is sitting at the right hand of the Father. Now someone doesn't sit down if there is still work to be done. Jesus has already finished the job of redeeming man from sin-we must each now simply believe in it personally for our own victory.

One day Jesus is going to get up from His throne and judge this whole world and all those who have rejected His finished work on the Cross. But as far as man's redemption is concerned, Jesus is finished with that. He has done all that needs to be done. That is why He is sitting at the right hand of the Father. Praise God!

WHY IS FREEDOM NOT BEING FOUND?

The Bible says, *"If the Son therefore shall make you free, ye shall be free indeed"* (John 8:36). The word *"indeed"* in the Greek is *"ontoos,"* which means *"truly, in reality, point of fact"* as opposed to what is pretended, fictitious, or false. Anything that presents itself as being a way for man to be set free that is not Christ and the Cross is fictitious, false and a lie from hell. There is only one way to be *"free indeed,"* and that is the way of the Cross!

King David said in Psalms 119:104, *"Through thy precepts I get understanding: therefore I hate every false way."* David said he hated a false way. Many churches today have stopped preaching the Cross and have turned to preaching a self-centered Gospel. We hear many sermons on how we can be more successful, more blessed, more prosperous, etc. But we don't hear many messages about the Cross or how we need to be crucified with Christ and die to self. Yet all the great revivalists preached the Cross and denial of self.

A.W. Tozer said, *"If I see aright, the cross of popular evangelicalism is not the cross of the New Testament. It is rather a new bright ornament upon the bosom of a self-assured and carnal Christianity. The old cross condemned; the new cross encourages it....the flesh, smiling and confident, preaches and sings about the cross; before the cross it bows and towards that cross it points with carefully staged histrionics, but upon that cross it will not die, and the reproach of the cross it stubbornly refuses to bear."* [1]

The Church must return to the Cross of the Bible. Let me repeat it again so that it really sinks into our minds and into our hearts. Any other way that is not the way of the Cross is a false way, and any time the Church moves away from preaching the Cross, it is going to fall prey to false teaching. The result will be people who are not living the victorious Christian life. That's why so many Christians today are caught up in sinful lifestyles and are bound by the world's vices. They don't realize that they have been led astray and that is why they are not experiencing the power of the Cross.

As a preacher once said, *"any time the Church leaves the Cross, they are not far from the golden calf."* Moses went up Mount Sinai to receive the Ten Commandments. While he was up there, when the people saw that Moses delayed to come down from the mountain, they gathered together and demanded that Aaron (the priest) build them a god of gold (Exodus 32).

The dividing line between the false way and the true victorious way is the Cross of Christ. The true Church will preach Christ and Him crucified as its foundational doctrine for everything (I Corinthians 2:2, 3:11). Doctrines that are centered on self, rather than Christ and the Cross, earmark the false way. The false way will make things such as blessings, faith, prosperity, holiness, personal disciplines, purpose, programs, church growth, etc. the main emphasis of its teaching. However, the root of all this teaching is a love of self. Today in the Church the *"golden calf"* is self and we are worshipping it.

The Bible predicted that in the last days *"men shall be lovers of their own selves"* (II Timothy 3:2). Unfortunately, that is for the most part where the Church finds itself today. We have become *"lovers of pleasure more than lovers of God"* (II Timothy 3:4).

WE NEED ANOTHER SPIRITUAL REFORMATION

The word *"reformation"* means *"a correction or improvement on what is corrupt or defective."* We must pray that the preachers of the Gospel come back to the Cross and preach that men must repent and believe in what Jesus did when He shed His blood to set us free.

Cross-Eyed

The power of the Holy Spirit to change a life can only be found through the message of the Cross. First Corinthians 1:18 says, *"For the preaching of the cross is to them that perish foolishness; but unto us which are saved it is the power of God."*

Ask yourself: why don't we see the power of God working through the Church as it did in the Book of Acts? I believe it is simply because we have left our *"first love"* (see Revelation 2:4). We need to come back to the old-fashioned, heartfelt, Holy-Ghost filled, devil-stomping preaching of the blood of Christ that sets men free! All the great preachers of old had the blood of Christ as the focus of their preaching.

The great Azusa Street Revival that occurred in 1906 in an old warehouse in Los Angeles, California, was used of God to birth a movement of God's Holy Spirit all over the world. Some called that revival the greatest of all revivals since the day of Pentecost. The Azusa Street Revival has literally touched the world. A New Testament translator, A.S. Worrell, declared that the Azusa work had rediscovered the blood of Christ to the church at that time.[2] Great emphasis was placed on the *"blood"* for cleansing, etc. A high standard was held for living a clean life, and it was only through the blood and the Holy Spirit that one could live it.

If a church is not preaching the message of the Cross, it has strayed from what the New Testament teaches and emphasizes. If a preacher is not preaching what Jesus preached or what Paul preached, then he is simply not preaching the Gospel.

A believer whose faith is not exclusively in Christ and what Christ did on the Cross is simply following a false way. Paul said to the Church of Galatia,

> *I marvel that ye are so soon removed from him that called you into the grace of Christ unto another gospel: Which is not another; but there be some that trouble you, and would pervert the gospel of Christ.*

> Galatians 1:6-7

The early Church's preaching was on Christ and the Cross. Understand when we say *"the Cross"* that we are referring to the resurrection as well, for you cannot separate the two.

> *The Bible says, "Now the Spirit speaketh expressly, that in the latter times some shall depart from the faith, giving heed to seducing spirits, and doctrines of devils; Speaking lies in hypocrisy; having their conscience seared with a hot iron" (I Timothy 4:1-2).*

So, it is imperative that every believer become *"CrossEyed"* and look only to the Cross for his victory over sin. The Cross is not just for salvation (justification), but it is for holy living as well (sanctification). The Cross is the foundation for everything you are and everything you do as a Christian.

> *"And ye shall know the truth, and the truth shall make you free."*

John 8:32

Chapter Five

Why Am I Living the Defeated Christian Life?

First Corinthians 9:24 says, *"Know ye not that they which run in a race run all, but one receiveth the prize? So run, that ye may obtain."*

Paul compares our lives as Christians to being in a race, and the Bible challenges us to run the race to win. But today many Christians are not winning or living victoriously. They are losing the race; and some have gotten so tired of defeat that they have quit and left the race altogether. Why?

Paul makes a bold but honest confession in Romans 7:15,

> *"For that which I do I allow not: for what I would, that do I not; but what I hate, that do I."*

I challenge you to take the Romans 7:15 experiment. Do you find that you do not do what you know to be right, but instead often walk according to the flesh and do the very thing that you hate? Read Romans 7:15 to believers at church or a Bible study and ask them to evaluate their lives honestly. Most believers are living the defeated Christian life and are in the same place Paul was in before he understood how to have victory.

If the bold confession of defeat made by the Apostle Paul is true of you, it does not have to remain that way! There is an answer to your dilemma. You don't have to live in defeat any longer.

Jesus said,

> *"The thief cometh not, but for to steal, and to kill, and to destroy: I am come that they might have life, and that they might have it more abundantly."*

John 10:10

So why don't more Christians live in victory? Why do we give in to the flesh, even after accepting the gift of salvation? Where is that abundant life that Jesus promised? Many Christians today are wondering, *"Why am I not experiencing victory? I am a believer; I know I'm saved; I love God with all my heart, but my sinful passions are still controlling me. Why?"*

The Bible promises, *"For sin shall not have dominion over you: for ye are not under the law, but under grace"* (Romans 6:14). This means the believer will not be dominated by sin. So, either the Bible is wrong, or we have missed something. We know the Bible is not wrong, so we must be missing something!

If the believer approaches the problem of sin in the wrong way, the outcome will be no different for the believer than for the unbeliever. The promise that sin will not have dominion over you is conditional. Notice what Romans 6:14 declares—we are not under the Law; we are under Grace.

If believers, after finding Christ as Savior, attempt to live righteous lives by keeping rules and regulations (by the law), they will not experience freedom over sin but will find that their sin natures (which still live in them) will again give them problems, will snatch away their victories, and will bring back defeat. They that live by the law—trying in their own strength to keep God's commandments—will see their sin natures reasserted to dominate their lives again.

However, if you will live your Christian life by trusting in God's grace, you will experience true freedom! When you are struggling with sin, ask yourself, *"Am I living under law or under grace?"*

Law Versus Grace

A Christian who is living under the law is doing the same thing an unsaved person does. He trusts in his good works to deliver him. Even though the believer is trusting in Christ to save him from hell, he is trying to live a holy life in his own good works. Attempting to walk in holiness with God by counting on good works will not result in living the abundant life Jesus promised. That is trying to live a sanctified Christian life by law, and it can't be done. This is defined as *"legalism."* Legalism is living by law rather than living by relationship. Living by law means the person is trying to produce his own victory.

Let me give you an example. A young man who is saved gets tempted in the area of lust. He gives in to that temptation and begins to look at pornographic movies, pictures, internet sites, etc. Now the Holy Spirit who lives within him convicts him. The man realizes that his lifestyle is grieving the Lord. He feels miserable and is trying with everything in him to stop, but he continues to fail. He has the Holy Spirit living within him, which means the power of God is available to him. But he doesn't know how the Spirit functions so he can gain victory over his problem with lust. He tries to stop, but continues to fail. Why? Because man cannot set himself free.

Although the young man may increase his devotional time in the Word and increase his prayer time to an hour or two every day, thinking this is what will take his sinful appetite away, he will still meet failure. He may become more active in his church and have an accountability partner (another man who can hold him accountable for his actions). These things will have some benefit to the person, as these are actions that every believer should take. But if he is trusting in these things to set him free, he will continue to meet failure in his walk with God.

This miserable state of failing and repenting, and failing and repenting brings some people to the point of total bondage, and they feel far away from the Lord. They get tired of struggling and feeling condemned. Many give up and stop trying, and some even lose their way with Jesus completely. Some will live in shame and condemnation. Others will simply take the position, *"That's just the way it is,"* not understanding that they don't have to live that way. Jesus provides a better way.

This is not an uncommon situation; it is one that is rampant in the Body of Christ. There are countless Christians who can't seem to gain the victory over sin. The bondages of sin may be different—your problem may not be lust but something else—but the struggle and the failure are the same.

What Is The Solution?

Let me give you some good news. There is a pathway of victory for every believer that is so glorious that it will remind you of how you felt when you were first saved!

First, let's realize that when it comes to living for God, failure is inevitable if we strive to defeat sinful desires and behaviors in our own strength. We are sure to fail if we think our victory over sin involves being more diligent or working harder at the Christian disciplines. Yes, the Bible tells us to *"work out your own salvation with fear and trembling"* (Philippians 2:12), and *"a man is justified by works, and not by faith only"* (James 2:24).

But we must ask ourselves the question, *"Who is it that produces the desire and the spiritual energy we need to perform the 'work'?"* Ask the question, *"Could I live the victorious Christian life before I received Christ?"* No. Of course we couldn't! We had no desire and no strength to even want to live the Christ-centered life. Before we got saved, we were sinners—and good ones at that. We could all say that before we were saved we were *"professional sinners."* What makes us think we can live the Christian life now?

You may say, *"Now I have the Lord in my life to help me,"* and you are right; but you must understand how the Lord helps you or you will have no victory over sin. Without a proper understanding of how to live the victorious Christian life, you will be left confused, frustrated and defeated.

Most Christians today are living the defeated Christian life because they are trying to live under a law (Old Testament) mentality. Jesus said,

> *Come unto me, all ye that labour and are heavy laden, and I will give you rest. Take my yoke upon you, and learn of me; for I am meek and lowly in heart: and ye shall find rest unto your souls. For my yoke is easy, and my burden is light.*

Matthew 11:28-30

This particular passage is one of the most inspiring statements Christ ever made! It lifts the burden of being religious and trying to gain God's acceptance. In this one statement, Jesus shows us all our religious efforts are unnecessary and a waste of human effort.

Jesus is stating that those who truly come to Him will find rest for their souls. The word *"rest"* in the Greek is *"anapausis,"* and it means *"to pause from labor."* It basically means taking a permanent vacation from trying to earn God's favor or trying to earn victory over sin!

Religion will tell you to be good so that God will accept you. But Christianity says, *"You can't be good, that is why you need a Savior."* Religion teaches you to work harder and do more to gain acceptance or victory. Christianity teaches that your victory is in Christ and the Cross. Religion instructs us to *"do, do, do"* but Christianity says, *"DONE, DONE, DONE!"*

Here is a chart to see if you are living under a religious mindset (law) or if you are resting in Christ and living under a grace mindset.

RELIGIOUS SYSTEMS—LAW

- I am trying to please God by good works—going to church, devotions, giving, praying, etc.

- I am trying hard not to sin.

- I am living by do's and don'ts—don't commit acts of immorality, don't lie, don't cheat, etc.

- I am looking to earn favor with God by being a good person.

- I am living my Christian life trying to keep the law (i.e. Ten Commandments).

CHRISTIAN LIVING—GRACE

- I am looking to the Cross as the means of God's favor for my life.

- I am trusting in the blood of Christ to justify and sanctify me.

- I am daily living by faith in Christ and Him crucified, and this keeps me in right relationship with God.

- I know that I have favor with God based totally on what Jesus did (on the Cross) and not what I do.

- I accept God's grace by faith in Christ. Every day I appropriate my faith in Christ and Him crucified, and I count on His grace to help me to live the Christian life through the power of His Spirit.

- I am yielding each day to the power of the Holy Spirit to produce holy living in me.

When a person becomes a Christian, he stops trying to earn God's favor; he simply receives it. He doesn't have to work for it. As Jesus said, *"It is finished"* (John 19:30). Hallelujah, Christ did it all! It is finished!

Jesus, by His shed blood, has made you acceptable in God's eyes, yet not you, but Christ who lives in you. But the question is, do you really believe that? Do you live like it? You may say you do, but your actions speak louder than your words.

I know a young girl named Katie who grew up thinking she had to try to please God, but the more she tried, the more she felt she had to do. Her efforts never seemed to be enough. She just continued to think she could never do enough to please Him. Even though she was a Christian, she felt far from the Lord. But one day the Lord gave her the revelation of His great love for her. She saw herself already accepted by God and saw that she didn't have to work to be loved by God—He already loved her. This revelation set her free in her Christian life. Now the Holy Spirit is alive and active in her life because she is not working from a law mindset; she is working from a grace mindset.

Here is another simple chart[1] to see if you are living your Christian life under law or under grace.

	LAW	*GRACE*
Your Focus:	Works	Christ and Him Crucified
Object of Faith:	Performance	Finished Work of Christ
Power Source:	Will Power	Holy Spirit
Result:	Failure	Victory

When a person lives under the law, he or she is constantly trying to earn God's favor. The object or focus of his faith is in his own performance. He depends on his own willpower to resist sin. All of this will only lead to failure. The Church can make all these rules: don't go to movies; don't wear long hair; have an accountability partner; don't smoke; don't drink; don't dance, etc. But this mindset falls under the category of law or legalism. The holy Christian life cannot be lived by outward rules and regulations. It must be written on the person's heart. You live for God from the inside out, not the outside in.

LIVING UNDER THE LAW

When we say *"the law,"* we are speaking of God's commandments, the do's and don'ts of the Christian life. Most Christians have been taught the Christian life through these do's and don'ts, and live under a *"faith in works"* mentality. If your Christian life is trusting in these works of the flesh, the defeated Christian life will be the result. A life lived by the law is a life cut off from the power of the Holy Spirit.

No one has ever lived a victorious Christian life by the law. It is impossible for man to keep the commandments. If we can't keep them, why did God give them to us in the first place? They were given to man for three main reasons:

1. God gave us the law so mankind would know His moral standards for living. The laws of God are the requirements that a holy God demands. The Ten Commandments show man what is right and what is wrong in God's eyes.

2. God gave us the law to show us how sinful we are and how much we need God. When we know what His standards are, we realize how far short we really have fallen. For example, Jesus said if you look at a woman with lust in your heart, it is as though you have committed adultery. The commandments have shown us how sinful we really are, in thought as well as deed.

3. God gave us the law to lead us to the Cross. A person does not know he needs to be saved until he first knows that he is lost. Most people today do not walk around thinking that when they die they are going to spend eternity in hell. Most think they are pretty good people and a loving God will not send them to hell. The law shows us that we have not kept the standards set by God, we are guilty of sin, and we need a Savior. This is why Jesus had to come and die for us.

The 10 Commandments in essence show us how sinful we really are.

> *Was then that which is good [God's law] made death unto me? God forbid. But sin, that it might appear sin, working death in me by that which is good; that sin by the commandment might become exceeding sinful.*

> Romans 7:13 comments added

The reason we are seeing America and Canada become more immoral is because the commandments of God (the Word of God) are no longer being held as the standard in our societies. But when the Word of God and the commandments of God are held as the standard, then sin will again become *"exceedingly sinful."*

Some time ago I was on a radio talk show warning young people about the movie *"Titanic."* A young girl called into the show and took exception with me. She didn't agree with my verdict that Christians should not see *"Titanic."* She said she had seen the movie and she didn't see anything wrong with it. I asked her if she knew that the Lord's name was used in vain over 12 times in the movie. She told me she hadn't even noticed. The more we are in the world and the less we are in the Word of God, the more we become desensitized by the things of the world.

Finally, feeling as though I was not getting anywhere with her, I gave one last attempt at reaching her. I asked the dear girl, *"WWJD? Do you think Jesus would spend $8 to sit in a theater and listen to His name blasphemed over 12 times, not to mention all the other immoral things that were depicted in that movie? Do you?"* There was a hesitation in her response and then, with a broken voice, she said, *"I guess not."* You see, when I matched the movie Titanic with the holiness of Jesus, it was then that the movie became *"exceedingly sinful."* This is what the law is meant to do.

> *Wherefore the law was our schoolmaster to bring us unto Christ, that we might be justified by faith.*

Galatians 3:24

WHY ARE MOST TEENS AND ADULTS FAILING GOD?

Why are the majority of Christian youth failing God? Statistics tell us that 74% of our Christian kids say they cheat on tests, 83% say they lie to teachers, 63% say they become physically violent when angered.[2]

The adults raising them do no better. They have similar problems such as lying to their spouses, cheating on their taxes, becoming violent in the home, etc. How could this be? One reason is a lot of Americans claim to know God when they really don't. Secondly, we have a lot of Christians who love God but are failing Him because sin has taken hold of their lives again.

Because most believers have never learned how to live the victoriously Christian life, they live the defeated Christian life. They continue to see the devil steal and destroy what God has for them. The Bible says, *"My people are destroyed for lack of knowledge"* (Hosea 4:6). Most Christians lack the knowledge of the Word of God that teaches them how to be free from sin.

So How Do I Live The Christian Life?

Let's go back to the last chart. The believers who look to the Cross and depend on God's grace daily will see the power of the Holy Spirit working in their lives, giving them the desire and strength to live the victorious Christian life. The object or focus of our walks with Jesus must be centered on what He has done on the Cross to defeat the forces of wickedness, and we must depend daily on His finished work. Christianity is not what we do, but what we know (what we believe).

Jesus said, *"And ye shall know the truth, and the truth shall make you free"* (John 8:32). We may ask, *"Free from what?"* Jesus' statement in John 8:32 came just a few verses after we read about the adulterous woman who was caught in sin. Jesus told her accusers that the one who was without sin could cast the first stone. They all had to throw their stones down and leave the Temple because they were all guilty of sin.

Many of us think that if we will read the Bible this much, or pray a certain amount of time each day, or bind the devil, or bind this spirit or that spirit, we'll be free. These things are good and should be done, but they are not what will bring freedom over the sin nature. Don't be deceived—it is not what we do that defeats the powers of darkness; it is what Jesus has already done for us on the Cross. Listen and learn the importance of I John 3:8,

> *He that committeth sin is of the devil; for the devil sinneth from the beginning. For this purpose the Son of God was manifested, that he might destroy the works of the devil.*

The believer must understand that Jesus Christ already destroyed the works of the devil two thousand years ago on the Cross. The question is, do you believe it—do you really believe it?

You may say, *"I do believe it,"* but then you live as though you have to go out and defeat the devil by your own works. How a believer deals with temptation and sin will tell him exactly where he has placed his faith. If someone talks about how he is trying to defeat a particular pattern of sin in his life, this particular believer has his faith more in what he does than in what Christ has already done.

Old Testament Example

The Book of Joshua gives us a great Old Testament example of God's power at work (Joshua, Chapter 6). Upon instructions from the Lord, the Jews marched around the city of Jericho once a day for six days, the priests carrying seven trumpets. On the seventh day, they marched around the city seven times, and at the precise moment, they made a long blast on the trumpets. Then all the people shouted, and the walls of Jericho fell down. This was God's strategy for the Children of Israel to take the City of Jericho. It happened just as God said it would. What is God trying to teach us through this Old Testament event?

At first glance, it looks like a silly thing for these men to do. But the lesson for us is huge. God is showing us that the way to defeat our enemies is not by might, nor by power, but by His Spirit (Zechariah 4:6). It didn't take great military might or political strategy that day to defeat Jericho. But it did take great faith. I mean, those men had to believe that marching, blowing some trumpets, and shouting was going to bring down the walls of a city. That took great faith on their part—not just to believe it, but to actually do it! True faith is always acting on what one believes.

It also looked silly when a teenaged boy holding a slingshot was standing in front of a nine-foot giant with the belief he was going to do what no one else in the entire Jewish army could do. You see, God likes to stack the odds so far against us that when we win the battles, there will be only one conclusion—it had to be God. The battle is won by faith, not by our own personal might or ability.

The Word of God teaches that our battles with sin are not won by trying harder or working for the victory; the victory is won by our faith. First John 5:4 says, *"And this is the victory that overcometh the world, even our faith."*

Chapter Six

Fighting The Wrong Battle

Romans 7:15 says,

> *For that which I do I allow not: for what I would, that do I not; but what I hate, that do I.*

The Apostle Paul makes a bold confession above. He confesses that he is living the defeated life and doesn't understand why; when he really wants to do right, he does not do it. Instead, he is practicing the very thing he hates.

I believe that if the truth be known, the majority of believers could make the same confession. There is a whole list of sins with which believers struggle: lust, sexual immorality, uncleanness, impure thoughts, drunkenness, idolatry, hatred, hostility, quarreling, anger, conceit, envy, jealousy, hatred, cheating, stealing, gambling, lying, and more.

This struggle over sin is common for us believers. The very thing we want to do, live righteously, is the thing we are not doing. However, the mere fact that it is a struggle is proof that we are saved. If we were lost, the sins with which we struggle would not bother us, at least not to the point of conviction that we are sinning against God.

The struggle in the heart of the believer is to change his or her behavior so that the lifestyle matches confession. Every believer at one time or another will face such a struggle.

> *"For the flesh lusteth against the Spirit, and the Spirit against the flesh: and these are contrary the one to the other: so that ye cannot do the things that ye would"*

> Galatians 5:17

Notice the word *"contrary."* The flesh and the Spirit are at war against each other within the believer's life. The flesh wants to go in one direction (the way of sin), and the Spirit wants to go in another direction (the way of holiness). This is the struggle that is within every born-again believer.

If Paul Can't Live It, Who Can?

Let's ask the question, *"If the Apostle Paul can't live the victorious Christian life, then who in the world can?"* I mean, Paul was a spiritual giant! He wrote nearly one third of the New Testament. He had a personal encounter with Jesus on the road to Damascus. He was dramatically saved and filled with the Holy Spirit. But in Romans, Chapter 7, this same man was failing God and didn't know why!

Through the Apostle Paul's struggle with sin, we will discover the secret to living a victorious life. The Bible doesn't tell us what Paul's sin was, but it really doesn't matter—sin is sin. Romans 7:18 says, *"For I know that in me (that is, in my flesh) dwelleth no good thing: for to will is present with me; but how to perform that which is good I find not."*

The will to live for God was present in Paul because he was saved and filled with the Holy Spirit (Acts 9:17-18). Before a person comes to Christ, he or she really has no desire to live for God. He enjoys sinning and is good at it. He may not like the consequences of sin, but he does enjoy the pleasures of sin (Hebrews 11:25). Once someone comes to Christ and is born again, the Holy Spirit comes in and places the desire to change within him. Sin is no longer fun and the person no longer wants to disobey God, he wants to please Him. That is why Paul said, *"...the will is present with me...."*

But also notice that Paul says *"nothing good dwells"* in his flesh. Paul recognized that his sinful nature was still present. Remember, when we get saved, God does not remove the sin nature. He simply dethrones (defuses or separates) it from dominating our lives. If God did remove the sin nature when we got saved, then we would not have any more problems with sin. But then we would not need God. God wants us to be dependent on Him, so He leaves the sin nature in us.

Paul's dilemma was that he realized that his flesh was still capable of sinning, but his new divine nature, (II Peter 1:4) given to him by

God, placed within him the will and power to fight against sin. As a result, he struggled and fought two natures. One nature wanted to live right and please God; the other nature wanted to sin. So the big question is, *"How did he conquer the sin nature or the sin problem?"*

If a sin is holding you captive—it may be lust, drugs, alcohol, gambling, anger, jealousy, an eating disorder, immorality, anxiety, depression or a thousand other things—and you don't know how to get the victory, look no further than the Word of God. God has given us the *"how to"* defeat sin in His Word.

ROMANS 7

There is a word in Romans 7 that will uncover Paul's main problem with trying to defeat sin in his life. It is the word *"I."* Paul uses the word *"I"* 33 times in Romans Chapter 7. At one time Paul's main problem was trying to defeat the sin nature or the sin problem through his own willpower and strength. The Bible calls this the work of the flesh. Circle the word *"I"* every time you see it in Romans 7 and see how Paul was trying to live the Christian life through himself. This is the main problem today with the modern gospel. Most of it is centered on *"self."* Many are struggling in their walk with God, because most of what is being preached today does not focus on the Cross. Instead, it focuses on self, which feeds our sin nature instead of starving it.

The word *"flesh"* could be described as our own ability, strength, or willpower. The Bible teaches that when we try to defeat sin in our own strength, we fall under law; we are trying to live by the commandments, and the Bible says this frustrates the grace of God. Galatians 2:21 says, *"I do not frustrate the grace of God: for if righteousness come by the law, then Christ is dead in vain."*

What does it mean to *"frustrate the grace of God"*? First of all, we must realize that Jesus Christ has already defeated sin on the Cross. His finished work on the Cross not only paid the sin debt that we could not pay, but it also broke the power of sin's grip, which we could not break. Christ has already won the victory over sin at the Cross. When we try by our own efforts to defeat any particular sin in our lives, we have actually circumvented the Cross and thereby frustrated the grace of God. He has already provided the answer to sin, which is faith in Christ and Him crucified.

It would be like me walking up to a total stranger and telling him I wanted to give him one hundred dollars, but he refused to take it on the grounds that he felt guilty taking the money because he has done nothing to earn it. I try to convince him that I just want to give him the money out of the kindness of my heart, but he continues to refuse my generosity on the basis that he doesn't receive handouts.

What has this man done? He has frustrated my grace. When we refuse to look to Christ and what He did on the Cross as the solution for sin, we frustrate God and His grace, and thereby quench the Holy Spirit's power. Now we are left to fight the giant (sin) on our own.

Understand, the flesh is no match for the devil or the sin nature. The devil will box your ears back every time. Some go down quicker than others, but all go down and receive the knockout punch. However, there is good news: the devil is no match for the power of the Holy Ghost.

If we have any biblical understanding at all, we will know that it is only by the Holy Spirit that we can have victory over sin. For Galatians 5:16 says, *"This I say then, Walk in the Spirit, and ye shall not fulfil the lust of the flesh."*

So the answer to the believer's struggle over sin is to walk in the power of the Holy Spirit. That is exactly what Galatians 5:16 is teaching us: it is by and through the Holy Spirit that the power of sin is broken. The prophet Zechariah declared hundreds of years before, *"Not by might, nor by power [human power], but by my Spirit, saith the LORD of hosts"* (Zechariah 4:6). The Christian's victory is found in the third person of the Trinity, God the Holy Ghost.

If it is by the Spirit that one walks in victory (and it is), then the big question is, *"How do I walk in the Spirit?"* How does the Holy Spirit operate and work in a believer's life to give one the victory over sin?

Let's look at the problem Paul had and why his own efforts were not only failing him but creating an even bigger problem. Romans 7:8 says, *"But sin* [the sin nature], *taking occasion by the commandment, wrought in me all manner of concupiscence. For without the law sin was dead."*

Now the words *"evil desires"* in Romans 7:8 is the Greek word *"epithumia,"* and it means *"a longing for what is forbidden."* It is to have a desire or lust after something that God forbids in His Word.

Paul is showing us that when he was trying to live for God by the law (by trying to keep the commandments), his sin nature was being stirred up and causing him to sin all the more. Why is that?

THE LAW CAUSES REBELLION TO SPRING UP

The heart of man is so evil that, when presented with rules and regulations, the sin nature in man wants to break those rules. The Bible says,

> *"There is none that doeth good, no, not one"* (Romans 3:12). Jesus said that we in and of ourselves are *"wretched, and miserable, and poor, and blind, and naked"*.

> Revelation 3:17

When I was in training to be a school teacher, we were taught that if you are in a room with a group of school children and you want them to go out a particular door in the room, just tell them the door that you want them to go out. Do not tell them to not go out the other door. The reason: there will be those who will want to go out the door you told them not to go out. Why? Because there is a rebel that lives within each and every one of us that wants to go against the rules.

This is why we have so many teenagers who have grown up in the Church and are living in rebellion against God—because most of them have been taught to follow God from a Law mentality and not a Grace mentality. The Bible says the law kills, but grace gives life.

Notice again, Paul discovered that when he tried to live his life by the law, he had more desire for the things that were forbidden in God's Word. So if a believer is trying to live his Christian life by the law or by his own strength, not only will he not succeed, but he will even break more laws. How evil is the heart of man!

If the believer attempts to live for God by means other than the Cross, he will be ruled by his evil desires. No matter how dedicated he might be otherwise, he will not be able to stop the process in that manner, but it will only get worse.[1]

The law cannot fix the problem of the sin nature; it only exposes it. This is what Paul is saying when he says, *"For without the law, sin was dead."* Until God gave the law, we did not even understand how unholy we were. But when He gave us His standards for life, then we saw what great sinners we really are.

TRYING TO LIVE THE CHRISTIAN LIFE BY THE COMMANDMENTS

This revelation that Paul discovered is so important for the believer to understand that it is worth repeating. Paul began his walk with Christ by trying to keep the Commandments in his own strength and will power. He found that in doing so, his old sinful nature was brought back to life and he began to die spiritually, totally defeated and helpless before God.

Romans 7:9 says, *"For I was alive without the law once: but when the commandment came, sin revived, and I died."* In this verse Paul explained his personal experience. He got saved and immediately enjoyed the new life of the Holy Spirit. But not knowing how to live for God, and not having yet received the revelation of the Cross, he reverted to trying to live for God by the law and found himself failing God.

Now you may be confused at this point, thinking, *"Doesn't God's Word say that we are to follow the Commandments?"* Yes, it does! Jesus said: *"If ye love me, keep my commandments"* (John 14:15).

John 14:21 says,

> *He that hath my commandments, and keepeth them, he it is that loveth me: and he that loveth me shall be loved of my Father, and I will love him, and will manifest myself to him.*

And I John 2:3-4 says,

And hereby we do know that we know him, if we keep his commandments. He that saith, I know him, and keepeth not his commandments, is a liar, and the truth is not in him.

The Word of God is commanding the believer to keep God's commandments, and this is where the believer gets tripped up. We must keep the commandments, but we must ask the question, *"How do I keep the commandments?"* Because if we go after this in the wrong way, we will end up defeated, frustrated, and ready to quit the Christian life. Unfortunately, many have actually done this.

Paul is pointing out that when he tried to live by the commandments, his sin nature revived. Now, friend, this is one revival in which you don't want to be involved!

Before Paul understood the Cross in terms of victorious living, he was going down the wrong pathway. He was trying to produce his own victory by keeping the commandments in his own willpower and strength. Not only did he find himself failing God, but the problem was actually growing worse and worse as his sin nature revived and came alive.

He wrote, *"And the commandment, which was ordained to life, I found to be unto death. For sin, taking occasion by the commandment, deceived me, and by it slew me"* (Romans 7:10-11). Paul was saying that the very commandments of God, which give us the moral standard of living to bring us life, deceived him and were killing him. Now, how could this be?

Well, the commandments weren't deceiving Paul; it was his own misunderstanding about the pathway of victory that was killing him. At one time Paul thought the way to live for God was to try, in his own best ability, to follow the Law. This is the deception that so many in the Church today believe. We think if we are just more committed to keeping the Christian disciplines, if we could just be more on fire and work hard to be righteous believers, then we would walk in victory over sin. We think if we just study enough, pray enough, keep our accountability partner close enough to us, stay under our covering, give enough, fast enough, or just plain try harder, then we will walk in victory. Well, not only is this mindset a deception and not the pathway to victory, but it will actually make the problem of sin in our lives even more out of control. Why? Because it is not God's prescribed pathway for victory. It actually is spiritual adultery!

SPIRITUAL ADULTERY

Read the beginning of Romans, Chapter 7:1-4. Paul compares a Christian going back to a law mentality to be as serious as a woman who cheats on her husband. Paul is stating the seriousness of a Christian who marries himself to Christ by grace through faith (the Bible calls us the Bride of Christ) and then goes back to living under the law. Paul is saying this is spiritual adultery. In Romans 7:4 the Bible says, *"Wherefore, my brethren, ye also are become dead to the law by the body of Christ; that ye should be married to another, even to him who is raised from the dead, that we should bring forth fruit unto God."*

We as Christians are married to Christ (spiritually speaking); we are no longer married or joined to the law. Christ has set the believer free from being under the law. Before Christ we were under the law; since we had sinned, we were law breakers, and under judgment. But because of the Cross and our faith in Christ and what He did for us at the Cross, we are now under grace and not the law.

HOW WOULD YOU FEEL?

A little boy is stuck in a burning building, and there is no one else who can save him but you. You rush into the burning building, risking your life to bring him out safely. As you go through the building, you are badly burned, causing you great physical pain. Finally, you reach the boy, who is on the fifth story of the building. By the time you reach him, it is impossible to return the way you entered the building. The only way out of the building is through the fifth story window. There is no fire escape out the window, and no one else is there to help you. So, with no other alternative, you wrap a cushion around the boy and cover him in a blanket. You take him in your arms and jump out the window! Miracle of miracles, the boy is saved. In fact, he is not even injured. However, the fall was too great for you, and you die of multiple injuries.

After saving the boy, your body lies lifeless on the ground. The boy gets up and suddenly remembers his teddy bear is still in the burning house on the fifth floor. So he runs right back into the burning building and is consumed by the flames. If you were looking from heaven, how would that make you feel? You sacrificed your life to save that little boy from the burning flames only to have him run right back into them. This would cause you great frustration, to say the least!

Now we can understand why God uses a term as strong as *"spiritual adultery"* to refer to a Christian going back to law after being saved by grace. It is an insult of the highest degree to the Cross of Christ when we circumvent the Cross and try to live the Christian life by the law through our own human efforts and our own works.

Every Christian must come to the conclusion that there is only one way to victory. There are not two ways, ten ways, or twelve ways; there is only one. Paul found out that nothing he was doing could set him free. He came to the end of himself; he was completely defeated.

I HAVE MET THE ENEMY, AND IT'S ME!

Paul is careful to point out that the problem in his life was not with the commandments, for they are holy; the problem was within him.

> *Wherefore the law is holy, and the commandment holy, and just, and good. Was then that which is good made death unto me? God forbid. But sin, that it might appear sin, working death in me by that which is good; that sin by the commandment might become exceeding sinful.*

Romans 7:12-13

The Law is like a mirror that shows us how evil we are. God gave the Ten Commandments—knowing that we could not keep them. They were given to us to show how *"exceedingly sinful"* we are

71

and how much we need Him. We must understand that the law has no power within itself to change us. It is simply a mirror or a tutor that leads us to Christ (Galatians 3:24).

The word *"tutor"* in the Greek is *"paidagogos"*, which means *"a tutor or a boy-leader, i.e. servant whose office it was to take the children to school."* The law's job is to show the sinner how exceedingly sinful he is, take that sinner to the Cross, and leave him there. That is the purpose of the law!

Paul saw the depth of the problem and why he was not experiencing victory over sin. He realized how sinful he really was. The sinful nature, even though it had been dethroned by the divine nature, was still causing him problems because he didn't understand how to appropriate his faith in the Cross and keep the sin nature down.

Romans 7:14 says, *"For we know that the law is spiritual: but I am carnal, sold under sin."* The word *"carnal"* here is *"arkikos,"* which means *"pertaining to the flesh."* These are the desires of the flesh. This is what I want to do to please my own fleshly desires. There are only two kinds of works: works of the flesh, or works of the Spirit.

The devil is good at lying to the believer, talking him into thinking that making a confession like Paul did in Romans 7 is not a confession of faith. Many Christians are taught to only make positive confessions such as, *"We are more than conquerors"* or *"I can do all things."*

However, have you ever noticed they never seem to finish the verse, therefore taking a particular Scripture out of the proper context, thus misinterpreting the verse? Notice what these verses really say, *"Nay, in all these things we are more than conquerors through him that loved us"* (Romans 8:37). *"I can do all things through Christ which strengtheneth me"* (Philippians 4:13). We must pay careful attention to whom it is that gives the believer victory over sin. It is Christ and Christ alone and not us, lest anyone should boast (Ephesians 2:9).

Paul is getting closer to revealing how his revelation of the Cross set him free. Romans 7 is providing a vivid, step-by-step picture for us to see how to be set free from all the vices of the evil nature. In Romans 7:15-20, Paul makes the confession that he was totally unable to live the Christian life due to the evil nature of his heart. It continued to stick up its ugly head to control Paul.

SPIRITUAL LAWS

Paul received more revelation concerning spiritual laws that God has put into place. Just as there are physical laws that govern our universe, there are also spiritual laws that govern the affairs of men. The word *"law"* in the Greek language is *"nomos,"* which means a *"governing principle that regulates the affairs of mankind."* It is vitally important that every believer understand these laws that have been set by God to regulate mankind's spiritual affairs.

1.   Law One—The Law Of Sin And Death

"I find then a law, that, when I would do good, evil is present with me."

Romans 7:21

Paul realized that there is an evil nature in him that is undeniable. It is a principle, and there was nothing he could do to escape the fact that he had a sin nature, and nothing he did in his own strength was going to rid him of it. Because of the law of sin and death, he was constantly presented with a problem that must be addressed.

The law of sin and death is the second most powerful law in the universe (Romans 8:2). This law requires that the consequence for breaking God's commands is separation from God—spiritual death. If we break God's commandments, we are going to die. We are going to be separated from God and His presence, and nothing could be as terrible as this!

2.   Law Two—The Law Of God

For I delight in the law of God after the inward man

Romans 7:22

The laws of God are very pertinent to our lives. These are the Ten Commandments (and hundreds of other commandments) made by God stating how man should live his life. As Ted Koppel

(ABC News analyst) once said, *"These are not the Ten Suggestions,"* meaning they are not open to debate.

God is going to judge this world based on His commandments. You and I are not going to be able to change them; they are Law!

3. Law Three—The Law Of My Mind

> *But I see another law in my members, warring against the law of my mind, and bringing me into captivity to the law of sin which is in my members.*
>
> Romans 7:23

The law of our minds is our desire as believers to fight sin. Every true believer in Christ has it in his mind that he must defeat the problem with sin. The *"law in my members"* is our sin natures warring with our minds, causing great anguish for every believer.

4. Law Four—The Law Of The Spirit Of Life In Christ Jesus

> *For the law of the Spirit of life in Christ Jesus hath made me free from the law of sin and death.*
>
> Romans 8:2

We have said that the law of sin and death is the second most powerful law in the universe. But Paul learned of a law that is greater than the law of sin and death—the law of the Spirit. When you understand the governing principle of how the Holy Spirit works, you will unlock the secret to the victorious Christian life.

The law of gravity was a law that no one could permanently defeat until approximately a hundred years ago. The law of gravity says that if you jump off a high building (or any building for that matter), you are going to fall. No matter how fast you flap your arms, you are going to come down. This law was known as unbeatable for about 6,000 years. Then God gave man the revelation, and man discovered a law that is greater than the law of gravity. It's called the law of aerodynamics. This law states when enough engine power and speed are created, one can defeat the law of gravity by getting off the ground and staying in the air.

The law of sin and death is like the law of gravity, and the law of the Spirit of life in Christ Jesus is like the law of aerodynamics. Once Paul discovered the law of the Spirit, he knew he could defeat the law of sin and death and thereby soar in his Christian life. What a revelation!

WHAT IS THE LAW OF THE SPIRIT?

Let's break down the law of the Spirit more precisely to give us more clarity. First of all, this law of the Spirit is called the *"Law of the Spirit of Life."* The Greek word for *"life"* is *"zoe,"* and means *"the state of one who is possessed of vitality or is animate."* The one who is filled with Holy Spirit Zoe will experience spiritual energy, enthusiasm, and power to live the Christian life.

When you see believers who are so filled with the love of God that they can't put their Bibles down, who are broken for a lost world, and are bold witnesses for Christ, you are looking at Christians filled with the Zoe of God. Nothing in this world can even remotely touch the experience of being filled with the Zoe of God.

This Zoe or Life of the Spirit is what defeats all the powers of hell and all the sinful tendencies of the sin nature. This Zoe will shut down your sin factory! It will defeat your sin nature and it will put the sign on the door *"out of business."* Glory to God and the Lamb forever!

The key to experiencing the Zoe of God is to know how the Spirit of Life operates or is governed within the believer's life. Let's go back to Paul. Thirty-three times Paul used the word *"I"* in Romans 7. All of Paul's own efforts to live the Christian life failed, and he came to the end of himself. Paul, in Romans 7:23, uses the word *"captivity."* He was a prisoner to his own lusts. He couldn't break out. He was trapped, and he gave a confession of complete and utter desperation in verse 24, *"O wretched man that I am! who shall deliver me from the body of this death?"*

The word *"wretched"* in the original Greek means *"exhausted from hard labor."* Paul was worn out trying to defeat his evil nature, finally came to the end of his miserable state, gave up and said,

Cross-Eyed

"Who can deliver me from this body of death?" Notice Paul did not say what can deliver me; he asked *"who."*

A twelve-step program won't deliver you from drugs, alcohol, or whatever other vice or sin you want to name. Your hope is in a Who! Your hope is in a person. Your hope and the hope of the world is in a man, the man Christ Jesus. First Timothy 2:5 says, *"For there is one God, and one mediator between God and men, the man Christ Jesus."*

The Pope does not have one ounce of authority over sin; Billy Graham isn't your answer; no program can deliver you; only Jesus Christ and what He has done through the Cross can deliver you from the law of sin and death and place you in His glorious light.

The phrase to be *"in Christ"* means that our faith is in Him and Him alone. He is the only one who can save us, deliver us and give us power over sin. To be *"in Christ"* means our total dependence is in Him and Him alone. To be *"in Christ"* means that our complete faith and trust for victorious living is in Him.

How Can I Be Delivered?

At the moment of desperation and defeat, Paul found how to be delivered from sin's grip. It is in the last verse of Romans 7 that we see that Paul had received the revelation of the Cross: *"I thank God through Jesus Christ."*

The Apostle Paul had found the answer! He found the secret to the *"mystery of godliness"* (I Timothy 3:16). His striving for victory over sin had ended, and he showed us that Christ and the Cross were the answer to his sin problem. He broke into joyful thanksgiving as he shared this new revelation.

Notice Paul did not say, *"I thank God for Jesus Christ,"* even though Jesus performed many miracles of healing, the feeding of 5,000 people, and teaching with wisdom and knowledge such as the world had never heard or known. However, none of these things is what set the captive free. It was what Christ did on the Cross that set mankind free, and Paul received this revelation in his moment of desperate need.

Paul uses the phrase *"through Jesus Christ."* This word *"through"* in the Greek is *"dia,"* which means *"to pass through or to cross over like in entering a gate or a door."* This word *"dia"* means that Christ and Him crucified is the door to victory over sin. It is only through the blood of Christ that we can cross over into to a lifestyle of victory (Ephesians 1:7). Paul found that door, crossed over that threshold and walked into victory. Then he shared it with the Romans (and us) through his letters.

When Paul said *"through Jesus Christ."* he was saying that the way to defeat sin is not by works or performance, but by the finished work of Christ on the Cross. Trusting in any other human effort, program, or thought is only a work of the flesh and would be classified as being under law. This approach will only lead to defeat.

The word *"death"* found in Romans 7:24 refers to the miserable condition of the Christian who is yet dominated by the evil nature from which he desires to gain victory (Wuest). In saying, *"the body of this death,"* Paul is referring to his body, where the sinful nature dwells. Meyer, a Bible commentator, rephrased it, *"Who shall deliver me out of bondage under the law of sin into moral freedom, in which my body shall no longer serve as the seat of this shameful death?"*

Many Christians think that deliverance comes through the laying on of hands or experiencing some emotional high. But for the believer in Christ, the Bible teaches that deliverance comes by the Spirit through proper understanding and faith in the deliverer, the Lord Jesus Christ. Jesus said,

> *The Spirit of the Lord is upon me, because he hath anointed me to preach the gospel to the poor; he hath sent me to heal the brokenhearted, to preach deliverance to the captives, and recovering of sight to the blind, to set at liberty them that are bruised, to preach the acceptable year of the Lord.*

Luke 4:18-19

Jesus said that deliverance comes through preaching. Whenever someone hears the preaching of the Word of God and believes it, freedom will come. The Bible says that *"it pleased God by the foolishness of preaching to save them who believe"* (I Corinthians 1:21).

Cross-Eyed

Therefore the message that is being preached is what is most important. The Message of Christ and Him crucified is the solution to man's stronghold of sin, and it is the only message that will set the captive free. When the Message of the Cross is preached under the anointing of the Spirit, men and women are going to be set free, for the Bible says, *"If the Son therefore shall make you free, ye shall be free indeed"* (John 8:36).

Chapter Seven

The Revolutionary Revelation!

But I certify you, brethren, that the gospel which was preached of me is not after man. For I neither received it of man, neither was I taught it, but by the revelation of Jesus Christ.

Galatians 1:11-12

Paul received the revelation of Jesus Christ directly from Him, and that is what this book is all about—the revelation of Jesus Christ, which could also be called the revelation of the Cross. God gave the Apostle Paul the revelation of the Cross so that Paul could share his discovery with the rest of the world. When God revealed the Cross to Paul, it not only set him free, but it has set countless millions of others free as well!

The devil does not fight any other revelation from God as furiously as he does the revelation of the Cross of Christ. He fights it fiercely because he knows that this revelation will set man free from his clutches.

Now, the word *"revelation"* in Greek is *"apokalupsis,"* which means a *"disclosure or a revealing discovery."* It means *"to uncover or to reveal something that has been hidden."* It also means a *"lifting of the veil."*

Imagine going to a play that has been highly recommended. You are in the theater, eagerly anticipating the performance. Although you really don't know what to expect, you have a sense that it is really going to be good. Suddenly, a drum roll begins; the curtain to the stage begins to lift, and finally you are able to see what is waiting beyond the veil.

The revelation of the Cross is this: Jesus provided the double cure. He not only paid our sin debts (salvation), He also broke the power of sin over our lives (to be made holy). The same faith that saved us is the same faith that will deliver us from our sins. What

Cross-Eyed

Jesus did on the Cross is for each of us personally, and must be received by each of us personally. The revelation of the Cross is not an answer to sin, it is the only answer to sin; there is no other.

Jesus has promised the victorious and abundant Christian life to every believer in Christ (John 10:10). It is imperative that every believer thoroughly understands the Message of the Cross. Paul said in I Corinthians 1:18, *"For the preaching of the cross is to them that perish foolishness; but unto us which are saved it is the power of God."*

The above verse reveals to us that if we want to experience the life-changing power of Jesus Christ, we must first understand and believe in the Message of the Cross. The Lord does not give this revelation to everyone, but only to those who fear Him and seek Him with all of their hearts. Psalm 25:14 tells us, *"The secret of the Lord is with them that fear him; and he will shew them his covenant."* The desperate and diligent searchers for God are in a great place to receive the revelation of the Cross and will find this precious jewel. Those who are proud and self-dependent will miss it.

Paul was at the end of his rope when God personally revealed the truth of the Cross to him. I am convinced that most true revelations from God come only through brokenness and defeat. The human heart is so proud and stubborn that it tries to live without God. But when a man comes to the end of himself, the Lord is there to rescue that weary and desperate soul. Psalm 107:27-28 says,

> *They reel to and fro, and stagger like a drunken man, and are at their wit's end. Then they cry unto the Lord in their trouble, and he bringeth them out of their distresses.*

Are you hungry and desperate for God to set you free from the control of sin?

I pray that for all of you who are weary from sin's destructive ways that this revelation will not only set you free, but you will become a conduit for many others to be free. I believe the revelation of the Cross will make you want to shout! It's a shout of victory. O, Victory! O, Victory! Christ has given me the victory!

The Power Of God That Sets Man Free

Paul said the Message of the Cross is the power of God (I Corinthians 1:18). Two thousand years ago, mankind viewed the greatest display of power ever known. God, through His Son Jesus Christ, set mankind free from the stronghold of sin and death. Jesus did this by shedding His blood and dying in a cruel and torturous fashion—on a wooden cross.

Christ willingly gave His life for lost humanity. No man or demon took it from Him, but He willingly laid it down. John 10:17-18 says,

> *Therefore doth my Father love me, because I lay down my life, that I might take it again. No man taketh it from me, but I lay it down of myself. I have power to lay it down, and I have power to take it again. This commandment have I received of my Father.*

Matthew 27:50 says, *"Jesus, when he had cried again with a loud voice, yielded up the ghost."* The word translated *"yielded up"* in the Greek language is *"aphiemi,"* and means *"to forsake, or to leave, or lay aside."* Jesus voluntarily gave, laid aside, His life.

The moment Jesus Christ yielded up His life on the Cross, the world experienced an incredible display of power. I believe that power was literally felt on every square inch of planet earth and probably throughout the universe.

The Bible tells us that there were five major cataclysmic happenings when Christ, God's only Son, died.

> *And, behold, the veil of the temple was rent in twain from the top to the bottom; and the earth did quake, and the rocks rent; and the graves were opened; and many bodies of the saints which slept arose,"*

Matthew 27:51-52

1. God Tore The Veil Of The Temple

The veil of the Temple, which the Jews hung in accordance with God's command, separated the Holy Place from the Holy of Holies where God's presence dwelt. It represented the separation between sinful man and a holy God.

Cross-Eyed

The high priest would enter the Holy of Holies only once a year on the Day of Atonement. He would spend much time in preparing himself before going beyond the veil. He would wash himself ceremonially to outwardly cleanse himself. He would also confess and forsake all sin in his personal life. If he went into the Holy of Holies with sin in his heart and life, he could die. Sinful man cannot enter into the presence of a holy God without dying. The veil was there to protect the people from God's holiness!

The high priest entered the Holy of Holies on the Day of Atonement to sprinkle the blood of the sacrifice on the altar at 9:00 am and 3:00 pm. The early morning blood was for personal sins, and the afternoon blood was for the nation's sin.

It was 9:00 am when they hung Jesus on the Cross, and it was 3:00 pm when Jesus gave up His spirit and died. At that precise moment (3:00 pm), God tore the heavy veil in the temple in two, from the top down to the bottom. Some scholars have estimated that the veil was four inches thick. The ripped veil signified that Jesus had paid the price for the sins of mankind! Hebrews 4:16 tells us, *"Let us therefore come boldly to the throne of grace, that we may obtain mercy and find grace to help in time of need."* Without sin separating us from God, we can boldly come into God's holy presence, all because Jesus' blood has atoned for sin once and for all time.

2. The Earth Shook

God's second incredible display of power when Jesus died on the Cross was an earthquake. Jesus' death on the Cross could have rocked the entire world!

This shaking of the earth's foundation represented a new day for mankind. No longer would men have to kill innocent animals for the remission of sin; the Lamb of God was slain and the price for sin was paid for all time. A great shift occurred in the heavens above and on the earth below. We were now moving in a new direction. The Old Covenant (Law), which God established with the children of Israel, was now finished; and the New Covenant, established by the blood of Jesus, had begun. It was and is a better covenant, an everlasting covenant.

Hebrews 8:6 says, *"But now hath he obtained a more excellent ministry, by how much also he is the mediator of a better covenant, which was established upon better promises."* This New Covenant is not made with the blood of bulls and goats, but with the precious blood of the Lamb of God. God freed the whole earth from sin's power through Jesus' sacrifice on the Cross.

3. The Rocks Split

When Jesus died on the Cross, the Bible says that the *"rocks split."* The cracking and splitting of the rocks could have been a result of the earthquake, but symbolically it could mean even more. Just as Moses struck the rock and water sprang forth (Exodus 17:6), the death of Jesus brought everlasting water (John 4:13-14) to a dry and thirsty world.

When the Roman soldiers nailed Jesus to the Cross, they split His hands and feet, and they had earlier split His back open when Pilate had Him scourged. Scripture compares Christ to a rock. In fact, Paul actually says that the Rock in the desert was Christ! *"For they drank of that spiritual Rock that followed them: and that Rock was Christ"* (I Corinthians 10:4). Psalm 40:2 says, *"He brought me up also out of an horrible pit, out of the miry clay, and set my feet upon a rock, and established my goings."*

Jesus said if we don't praise the Lord, the stones will cry out (Luke 19:40). When Jesus died on Calvary, the stones began to pop and crack as if to say, *"Praise God; mankind can be free!"* Oh, the Power of the Cross—there is nothing else like it!

4. The Graves Opened

The Scripture in Matthew says that when Jesus died on the Cross, the graves of the saints who had passed on before were opened. This represents that through the crucifixion of Jesus, the death sentence of sin was paid in full. The Bible says that the wages of sin is death (Romans 6:23), but because of Christ and what He did on the Cross, the wages have been paid.

5. Many Bodies of The Saints Arose

Cross-Eyed

The dead bodies of many of the saints which slept arose (Matthew 27:52-53). This is an interesting point. Dead people were brought back to life, not on the day Jesus rose again, but on the day that He paid sin's debt! However, they were not permitted to leave their graves until Jesus rose on the third day.

Matthew 27:52 shows us that victory over death was paid in full at the Cross on Calvary; the Cross of Christ defeated the greatest enemy of man-death. First Corinthians 15:55 says, *"O death, where is thy sting? O grave, where is thy victory?"*

There is no power even remotely comparable to the life-changing and life-transforming power of the Cross of Christ. When you see it and depend on it exclusively, it will save and deliver you. Then and only then will you find true freedom.

Listen to the words of the Roman centurion and those around him who viewed the events of the Cross.

> *Now when the centurion, and they that were with him, watching Jesus, saw the earthquake, and those things that were done, they feared greatly, saying, Truly this was the Son of God.*

Matthew 27:54

This Roman guard could very well have been one of the men who put the spikes in the hands and feet of Jesus, nailing Him to the Cross! There were no atheists at the Cross of Calvary. The power of the Cross literally rocked the world, and it is still rocking the world some two thousand years later!

THE REVELATION OF WHO JESUS IS

Jesus asked the disciples, *"Whom do men say that I the Son of man am?"* And they said, *"Some say that thou art John the Baptist: some, Elias; and others, Jeremias, or one of the prophets"* (Matthew 16:13-14). Then Jesus asked them, *"But who do you say that I am?"* And Simon Peter answered and said, *"Thou art the Christ, the Son of the living God"* (Matthew 16:16).

Jesus answered Simon Peter and said,

> *And Jesus answered and said unto him, Blessed art thou, Simon Barjona: for flesh and blood hath not revealed it unto thee, but my Father which is in heaven. And I say also unto thee, That thou art Peter, and upon this rock I will build my church; and the gates of hell shall not prevail against it.*

Matthew 16:17-18

The whole Church of Jesus Christ is established upon the revelation of who Jesus is and what Jesus did. Man cannot reveal this to an individual, only the Father can. So let's pray that He will make the revelation of the Cross known to you.

I believe that to receive this revelation from God, you must be a dry and thirsty soul who wants to know God in a greater way and who wants to live a life that is pleasing to Him. I think it is important at this point that we stop, pray and ask God to give you the revelation of the Cross. You might say that you already have it. Well, if you are truly born again, then that is true as it relates to salvation from hell.

However, ask yourself this question, *"Do I have the revelation of the Cross for my sanctification?"* Are you living the victorious Christian life because you believe what Christ did on the Cross? Let's pray that God gives you that revelation of the Cross.

Dear Heavenly Father, I come to You in Jesus' name. I humbly ask You to supernaturally make known to me the revelation of the Cross. Show me the pathway of victory that You gave to Paul so that I can please You in all that I say and do. In Jesus' name, I pray. Amen!

Chapter Eight

The Message Of The Cross Is The Answer

Jesus came to bring freedom to the whole human race—freedom from hell, freedom from sin, and freedom from the devil's control over our lives. Mark the following verses in your Bible:

- John 8:32—*"And ye shall know the truth, and the truth shall make you free."*

- John 8:36—*"If the Son therefore shall make you free, ye shall be free indeed."*

- Galatians 5:1—*"Stand fast therefore in the liberty wherewith Christ hath made us free, and be not entangled again with the yoke of bondage."*

Freedom from sin and the devil's stranglehold is found in no other place than at the Cross. At the Cross, Jesus defeated the principalities and powers that held you in bondage. When Jesus died, He paid the sin debt and He broke the grip Satan had on the human race. Satan was holding your offenses against you—your sins. Like a prosecutor in a courtroom, he was holding up all the laws of God that you had broken, and he was telling God that you were guilty.

But now in Christ Jesus ye who sometimes were far off are made nigh by the blood of Christ.

Ephesians 2:13

Your sin had pushed you away from God, but the blood of Christ has brought you near to Him. The Bible teaches that for a guilty party to be freed from sin, there must be the shedding of blood—and that blood must be perfect In other words, the penalty for sin is death (Romans 3:23). Someone has to pay that penalty. Either the guilty sinner will die, or someone has to die in his place. But the one who dies in his place must be guiltless of any crimes (sin), or the sacrifice will not be accepted.

Second Corinthians 5:21 says, *"For he* (God the Father) *hath made him (Christ) to be sin for us,* (the offering for sin) *who knew no sin;* (Jesus was perfect and never sinned) *that we might be made the righteousness of God in him"* (words in parentheses added).

The blood that was shed on Calvary's Cross by Jesus Christ has set us free from Satan's stranglehold. Hebrews 9:22 says, *"And almost all things are by the law purged with blood; and without shedding of blood is no remission."* It was Christ's perfect blood that was shed that has provided the remission of sin.

The devil hates the Cross vehemently, and he will do everything he can to keep the world from the Cross. He will try to confuse the believer into thinking the power of the Cross is not sufficient to break the power of sin. He will lie to the believer and try to mislead him.

We must realize that many false teachers have come—especially in the last fifty years—to deceive the body of Christ and to keep us either uninformed or misinformed as to all the benefits of the Cross. Many in the Church today don't study their Bibles. They just have enough knowledge to save them (if they have that), but they know very little about the Cross in terms of sanctification (holy living).

Let's look at two important scriptures in the Bible that give the truth of the Cross so we can know completely what Jesus did for us. These verses unveil the truth to the believers so Satan can no longer keep the revelation of the Cross veiled from our eyes.

Luke 9:23 says, *"And he said to them all, If any man will come after me, let him deny himself, and take up his cross daily, and follow me."*

Many Christians misinterpret this verse by thinking that it is saying that we must suffer (bear a cross) to be a follower of Jesus. Even though being a Christian will bring trials, tribulations, and persecution, this is not what the verse is proclaiming. Let's take a closer look at what Jesus is saying:

1. Deny Yourself

Jesus is saying that to be a follower of His, that person must first *"deny himself."* He must deny or refuse his own ability, willpower, self-will, and strength—he must depend exclusively and totally on Christ. Many Christians are attempting to live the Christian life in their own strengths and abilities. This is why they are failing.

2. Take Up Your Cross

Taking up our Cross does not mean that we believers must go through suffering to be acceptable to God, or that through suffering we earn our stripes. No, taking up our Cross means placing our faith in Christ and Him crucified, and trusting exclusively in what Christ did at the Cross. We must take up (have faith in) the finished work of what Christ did at the Cross.

3. Daily

Our lives are lived one day at a time. The only way that we are going to live a victorious Christian life is by renewing our faith in Christ and Him crucified on a daily basis. It only takes one day for our faith to move away from Christ and the Cross and to experience failure. That is how much we need God. We can't even make it one day without His power strengthening us.

4. And Follow Him

Once we have denied our own willpower and abilities and are looking exclusively to the Cross of Christ for our victory on a daily basis, then we will experience the power of His Spirit to truly follow Christ.

SALVATION—WHAT AM I REALLY SAVED FROM?

"For by grace are ye saved through faith; and that not of yourselves: it is the gift of God" (Ephesians 2:8). This Scripture tells us how we are saved. We are going to look at the three key words in this passage—grace, saved, and faith—to better understand how we obtain victory over sin's penalty and sin's power.

SAVED

This word *"saved"* means more than most Christians understand, and this is where Satan veils the message of the Cross. The word *"saved"* in the Greek is *"sozo,"* which has two main definitions:

- The spiritual and eternal salvation granted immediately by God to those who believe in Christ. When we believe in Christ, God saves us from the eternal damnation our sins have earned. We've been rescued from hell!

- The present experience of God's power to deliver from the bondage of sin.

Because of what Christ did on the Cross, we are free or saved from the powers of sin controlling our lives here on earth. At the Cross, Jesus provided the double cure for sin. He not only paid the sin debt, but He also broke the sin grip. Glory to God!

As believers in Christ and Him crucified, we are not only on our way to heaven because of the Cross, but we can experience freedom from sin's control here on earth. Now that is worth shouting about!

So, why are so few Christians experiencing sozo, saved from sin's power? The simple answer to that question is they may be trusting in what Christ did at the Cross (if they are truly born again) to save them from hell when they die, but they are not trusting in what Christ did at the Cross to deliver them from sin right now.

When we say, *"I am saved,"* we should no longer think of our salvation as only rescuing us from hell (although that would have been enough); but we should also think, *"I am also saved from the power of sin controlling and ruling my life today."*

Why don't we just stop and have a Holy Ghost party on this truth right now? Oh, praise God! Let's take a moment and tell the devil that he was defeated at the Cross and we are no longer in bondage to the fear of death or the control of sinful desires. We are free from the devil's trappings, all because of the blood of Calvary. *"If the Son therefore shall make you free, ye shall be free indeed"* (John 8:36). This is why Jesus came!

Grace

"Grace" means *"undeserved or unmerited favor."* Grace should be thought of as the generosity of one person to another. It is when someone gives things away to someone else, even though he has done nothing to deserve them, and actually has done things that deserve punishment instead of blessing. But the love of that person is so great that, without any reason to give—except the mere fact of unconditional love—he extends gifts so abundantly that it staggers the mind.

Realize this one fact: an unholy person can never do anything that warrants acceptance from a holy God. We receive our salvation not because we deserve it or because we have earned it, but because of God's amazing grace. This mere fact removes any bragging rights. We have done nothing to deserve it. To the contrary, we have actually earned the opposite!

We receive grace and mercy from the Lord. The difference between grace and mercy is this—grace is receiving from God what we don't deserve; and mercy is not receiving from God what we do deserve. We believers receive a free ticket to heaven and the power to live in victory over sin, which we do not deserve. We don't go to hell and live in the control of sin's power, which we do deserve.

Faith

The victorious Christian life is a gift. It cannot be earned. We receive God's power to turn away from sin *"by grace through faith."* Faith is the means by which we receive God's free gifts. But the question must be asked, *"Faith in what?"* It must be faith in Christ and Him crucified or it isn't the true faith (I Corinthians 2:2, Galatians 3:1, 6:14).

There was a man in the Bible named Bartimaeus. He was a blind beggar and had nothing to give Jesus. But Jesus healed him of his blindness based on two things. He cried out for Jesus to have mercy on him, and he had faith that Jesus would heal him (Mark 10:46-52). This is all it takes to be a follower of Jesus. Just cry out to Him and believe, and He will do great and mighty things in our lives.

That blind beggar is a representation of all of humanity. We cannot see as we ought to, and we are not able to cure our own blindness. We are only blind beggars, crying out for God's healing power.

When Bartimaeus heard it was Jesus walking by, he began to offer his cry for help. The people around him told him to quiet down, but the Bible says he cried out all the more. The world will always tell the person to quiet down and don't make a scene; don't become too fanatical. But if Bartimaeus had listened to that crowd, he would have never received his miracle. God moves through people's faith. The faith of man is nothing more than a cry for Jesus to help him and a belief that He can.

You Are On The Winning Team—If You Are In Christ

"And you, being dead in your trespasses and the uncircumcision of your flesh, He has made alive together with Him, having forgiven you all trespasses, having wiped out the handwriting of requirements [the Law] that was against us, which was contrary to us. And He has taken it out of the way, having nailed it to the cross. Having disarmed principalities and powers, He made a public spectacle of them, triumphing over them in it."

Colossians 2:13-15

The word *"triumphing"* in the Greek is *"thriambeuo,"* which means *"to make an acclamatory procession,"* a victory celebration.

Every year the team that wins the World Series has a ticker tape parade where fans celebrate their team's triumph. In Biblical times when an army defeated another nation, they would often capture the defeated king. The day after the victory, the victors would hold a parade with the king of the defeated nation placed on a cart, stripped down naked. He would be tied to a post and paraded down the road past the victorious king perched on his victory seat. The people would cheer in victory as their king watched the defeated king being paraded in shame.

This is the same word picture the Bible uses to describe to us that at the Cross Jesus Christ made a public show of the devil and all his demons, triumphing over them. The next time the devil comes knocking at your door, just tell him, *"Devil, let's go to the show."* Take him to the Cross and remind him that because of the Cross, he has been stripped naked by Christ and now he is paraded down the street defeated. Remind him that at the Cross, he was made a public spectacle by what Jesus Christ did there.

Every believer has been set free from sin's power. That should make all believers in Christ bold witnesses to a lost world. We are not going to hell, and we are not in bondage to any sin that Satan can throw our way because we are redeemed by the blood of the Lamb that was shed on the Cross.

There are so many today who are in bondage to sin. Sin is destroying their marriages, their families, their futures and their lives. But we have the answer that can set them free and save their lives. It is the Message of the Cross. Every believer should want to shout it from the rooftops. We have the message that can cure humanity.

Ephesians 1:7 says, *"In whom we have redemption through his blood, the forgiveness of sins, according to the riches of his grace."* The word *"redemption"* means *"to release on payment of ransom."* You and I were held hostage by the devil because of sin, but on the Cross Jesus Christ paid the ransom so our souls could be set free! We are redeemed! We should thank God every day for the Cross of Christ.

THE MAIN MESSAGE OF THE BIBLE

From Genesis to Revelation, we can see the Cross. The Bible begins with the emphasis on the sacrifice (Genesis 3:21, 4:4), and the Bible ends with the emphasis on the sacrifice. In Revelation the Bible says,

> *And he shewed me a pure river of water of life, clear as crystal, proceeding out of the throne of God and of the Lamb. In the midst of the street of it, and on either side of the river, was there the tree of life, which bare twelve manner of fruits, and yielded her fruit every month: and the leaves of the tree were for the healing of the nations.*

And there shall be no more curse: but the throne of God and of the Lamb shall be in it; and his servants shall serve him:

Revelation 22:1-3

John received the vision of heaven; notice the tree of life. The tree of life, which was in the Garden of Eden, is now in Heaven. The Bible says that this tree of life represents life eternal (Genesis 3:22). When Adam and Eve disobeyed and ate from the tree of good and evil, it brought death to them and to the whole human race. But when Christ died on the *"tree"*—the Cross—He repurchased life for all of humanity. First Peter 2:24 says Jesus *"bare our sins in his own body on the tree, that we, being dead to sins, should live unto righteousness: by whose stripes ye were healed."* At the tree, Adam and Eve lost their way with God, but at the tree of Calvary, man found his way back to God.

The word *"Lamb"* was used twice in these three verses. This is speaking of Jesus and what He did on the Cross for us. John the Baptist, when first seeing Jesus, called Him the Lamb of God (John 1:29). Jesus Christ and what He did on the Cross is the central theme, not only of the Bible, but of heaven for all eternity.

THE FALSE GOSPEL

In today's modern Church, the Gospel has been so perverted that many do not know or cannot clearly explain what the Gospel is. All false doctrine will usually fall into two main categories:

1. Denying the deity of Jesus Christ. Teaching that Jesus, although He is the Son of God, is not God.

2. Mixing grace and law, or faith and works together.

In Galatians 1:6-7, Paul said the following,

I marvel that ye are so soon removed from him that called you into the grace of Christ unto another gospel: Which is not another; but there be some that trouble you, and would pervert the gospel of Christ.

The Judaizers (Jews who taught the Mosaic Law) of that day were instructing the people who believed in Jesus that they were

94

still under obligation to keep the law even though they had come to faith in Christ. The Judaizers would definitely fall into the second category.

Paul was rebuking the Galatians for turning away from the true Gospel to another gospel, one perverted by adding Law to Grace. We know the true Gospel is the Gospel of Christ (Galatians 1:7). The true Gospel is all about Jesus Christ and Him crucified!

First Corinthians 15:1-2 reads,

> *Moreover, brethren, I declare unto you the gospel which I preached unto you, which also ye have received, and wherein ye stand; By which also ye are saved, if ye keep in memory what I preached unto you, unless ye have believed in vain.*

Paul reminded the Corinthian Church that the Gospel that he preached brought salvation and that they were to keep that Gospel in their memories. Satan will always try to distort the true Gospel and move the believer away from the true faith.

When somebody asks you *"What is the Gospel?"*, you can tell them straight up that it is Jesus Christ and Him crucified, buried, and risen from the dead. That is the Gospel of Christ!

It is your personal faith in the Gospel of Christ that saves you from eternal wrath and dominion of sin. If you will believe that Jesus Christ died on the Cross for your sins, that He was buried for you, and three days later He was raised from the dead to give you newness of life, you will be saved. It is a personal faith in the Gospel of Christ that makes you righteous and saves you from eternal judgment.

Paul said anyone who adds to or takes away from the true Gospel should be excommunicated (prevented from fellowshipping with true believers). In Galatians 1:8 Paul says, *"But though we, or an angel from heaven, preach any other gospel unto you than that which we have preached unto you, let him be accursed."*

The Amplified Bible defines the word *"accursed"* as meaning *"anathema"*—devoted to destruction or doomed to eternal punishment. It is a serious crime indeed to pervert the Gospel of Christ. It is serious, for we are dealing with eternity here—the place where men and women will live forever and ever. Changing the Gospel can send men to hell!

GOSPEL OF CHRIST

The Bible says, *"And Jesus went about all Galilee, teaching in their synagogues, and preaching the gospel of the kingdom, and healing all manner of sickness and all manner of disease among the people"* (Matthew 4:23).

What is the Gospel of the Kingdom that Jesus preached? It is not only salvation for the soul, but it is also healing for the body. Even though there are those who claim that healing passed away with the apostles, the Word of God says the very opposite. The Gospel of the Kingdom is all that Christ purchased at Calvary and through the resurrection. It is the healing of the soul, mind and body. Jesus did a complete work at the Cross.

Regrettably, most of that which presently passes for the Gospel is not the gospel at all, but is a watered-down, compromised version. This *"modern gospel"* lacks truth and the power of the Holy Spirit. We must come back to the heartfelt, true-blue, devil-stomping, Holy-Ghost-filled Gospel. We must earnestly contend for the faith which was once delivered unto the saints (Jude 3). We must preach the same Gospel that was preached in the Book of Acts: Christ crucified and risen from the dead (see the Book of Acts).

Chapter Nine

How Do I Walk In The Spirit?

Having received the revelation of the Cross, Paul now understands how the Holy Spirit works, and he goes on to write the great eighth chapter of Romans. The Apostle shares his insight on how to live the victorious Christian life.

Paul said, *"There is therefore now no condemnation to them which are in Christ Jesus."* Paul does not base his *"no condemnation"* statement upon the believer's moral conduct but on his position in Christ. Paul saw that his position in Christ had liberated him from the compelling power of the evil nature. It made him a partaker of the divine nature, a new inner condition producing a life of obedience to His commandments.[1] Paul was operating in faith and not in works. He was now under Grace and not Law.

Paul obviously had lived under condemnation from the evil one for his hypocritical lifestyle. The devil torments struggling Christians, hoping that their frustration and guilt will lead them to give up. Unfortunately, he succeeds in many cases.

But Paul saw the complete victory in the Cross, and he stopped looking at himself and what he had to do to live the life of a Christian. This misplaced faith had led to defeat and condemnation. He now had his eyes on Jesus, on the One who is perfect and never sinned. Christians who are walking in defeat have shifted their eyes away from Christ and the Cross to themselves and their own vain efforts to defeat sin.

The believer must come back to his first love and get his eyes back on Christ. A person who is focused on Christ and the sacrifice He made to redeem him will begin to sense a new conviction to live for God and not to fulfill the lust of the flesh.

GOSPEL OF SELF

Much of the preaching and teaching today in the modern Church is centered on self—how a believer can be more successful, more prosperous, more satisfied, etc. But the Bible is not centered on self. In fact, the Bible tells us to crucify self (Galatians 2:20). Jesus said whoever wanted to be His follower must first *"deny themselves"* (Luke 9:23).

On Christian TV or in your Christian bookstore, you will often see great emphasis on improving self. But the focus of Christianity should not be on self but on Christ. The discerning Christian can spot the false gospel of today. Remember, it was Satan's original plan with Eve to get her eyes off God, cause discontentment within her heart, and plant the thought that she could be more than what she was. The serpent said to Eve when she ate of the tree of good and evil, *"you will be like God"* (Genesis 3:5).

Satan has not changed his tactics. He is still lying to us and trying to cause discontentment within our hearts. He wants our eyes to be on ourselves. He wants us to be constantly striving to be more than who we are. He wants the preacher to focus on how many people he has in his church and what he can do to grow numerically. He wants the speaker to focus on how much money he can make through his speaking ability. He wants the writer to focus on how many books he can publish. He wants the singer or band to keep pumping out new albums for the sake of status and financial success. He wants the Christian to think that if he improves himself, he will achieve more, earn more, and feel better about himself.

But the Bible teaches us to die to self and allow Christ to grow stronger in our lives so that the world will see Him and glorify Him. Paul says to those who are in Christ, meaning their faith is in Him, that there is no condemnation because they are walking in victory over sin. The Holy Spirit is flowing and they have changed the way they are walking. The key is being *"in Christ"* by faith. It is our position in Christ and not our performance that gives us victory over sin.

The Revelation Of The Cross

When a person gets the revelation of the Cross, as Paul did, that person's walk changes. Why? Because the river of the Spirit is flowing. The desire to fulfill the fleshly lusts has been broken.

If you are in bondage to sin right now, your answer is the Message of the Cross. It doesn't matter what the sin is, your only answer is to believe totally and completely in what Jesus did at the Cross to break your addiction. At the Cross, Jesus defeated that sin and its power over your life. If you're a believer in Christ, you don't have to work to free yourself from your addiction; you just have to believe you have already been freed from it because of what Jesus Christ did on the Cross 2,000 years ago. He took your individual sin with Him to the Cross and nailed it there. His shed blood releases you from the power of that sin. The big question is: *"Do you believe it?"*

A Powerful Example

A woman who came to our church had many problems; after a service she came to me for help. She had married and then divorced the same man twice. Now she was contemplating marrying him for a third time. While a little girl, her stepfather had abused her. Every time she married and lived with this man, his mannerisms would remind her of her abusive stepfather. These memories would send her into deep depression and she would shut down, which caused all kinds of problems in her marriage.

She had gone to counseling for many years. The best secular psychologists available counseled her, but that didn't set her free. Many different Christian counselors tried to help, but she was still in bondage to her horrible past.

I sat down with this dear lady and her ex-husband to listen to her problems. One of my first questions was, *"What is your counselor saying to you?"* She was at the time seeing one of the supposedly best Christian counselors in the area. She said, *"Well, he says that I'm doing better and that I am getting closer to praying the prayer of deliverance."*

Cross-Eyed

I said to that dear sister, *"You don't have to get ready to pray the prayer of deliverance, you already are delivered by what Christ did for you on the Cross 2,000 years ago. YOU JUST HAVE TO BELIEVE IT!"*

I then took the next 20-25 minutes and walked her through the Scriptures (mainly Romans, chapters 6 through 8), showing her how Jesus had defeated every sin and bondage at the Cross. I told her that her battle over her past was not won by what she could do to overcome it, but by believing what Jesus did on the Cross for her. Her victory would not come through something she did, but her victory was completed by the finished work of Christ on the Cross. I told her that it was her faith in what Christ did on the Cross that would give her the victory over depression, pain and bitterness.

After this we prayed, and while praying the Lord gave her a revelation of the Cross. She actually had a vision of a wooden cross coming toward her and piercing her heart. She saw the Cross healing her broken and bitter heart. At that moment, this dear lady was instantly delivered. What 20 years of counseling couldn't do, Jesus did in 20 minutes—once she properly understood and believed what Christ did on Calvary for her. The revelation of the Cross set her free. Glory to God! This woman is one of the most faithful women in our church, and she has been inspired to write a book about her deliverance. Hallelujah!

We are not delivered by what we do, we are delivered by what we believe! John 8:32 says, *"And ye shall know the truth, and the truth shall make you free."* The glorious truth of Jesus Christ and Him crucified is the answer to all of our problems, bondages, and evil vices that try to latch on and destroy us.

This may seem too easy of an answer. The Gospel is easy to understand, but it is hard to believe. Our carnal minds have been trained since we were children that we have to do something to be saved and to be delivered.

If you are struggling with sin and it is destroying your walk with God—and maybe it is destroying your marriage—then this book is presenting the answer to your problem! But you must receive the revelation from God and truly believe it. When Peter made the confession that Jesus was the Christ, the Son of the living God, Jesus responded by saying, *"flesh and blood hath not revealed it unto thee, but my Father which is in heaven"* (Matthew 16:17).

Everyone Needs A "Wretched Man" Moment

Just like Paul, every person needs a wretched man moment. You must come to the end of yourself, throw up your hands, and tell God you have given up trying to live the Christian life or trying to be a faithful follower of Christ in your own strength. All of your efforts have fallen miserably short.

Right now many Christians are living a hypocritical lifestyle. They go to church and people see that they are Christians—but deep down most of them are fighting a losing battle with sin. They are living in a cycle of sinning and repenting, sinning and repenting. If the truth were known, most Christians' lives would not reflect the victorious Christian life that Jesus died to give them.

However, if we will learn the proper pathway to victory outlined in the Bible, then—and only then—we will experience true victory over sin. We must get the same revelation of the Cross that Paul got, or there is no hope of living in freedom over sin. Here is a short outline of the Biblical pathway to deliverance from sin.

1. Humble Yourself—Admit that you cannot live the Christian life. Come to your wretched man moment. The church in Laodicea held on to their pride and thought that because they had money, they were doing good. But Jesus gave them the truth about themselves. *"Because thou sayest, I am rich, and increased with goods, and have need of nothing; and knowest not that thou art wretched, and miserable, and poor, and blind, and naked"*

Revelation 3:17

God wants us to admit that we need Him and that we need Him every day. Pride is a terrible thing; it says *"I don't need anyone's help, I can make it on my own."*

Cross-Eyed

Humbling yourself and admitting your weakness and inability to set yourself free will draw the Holy Spirit to you and bring His amazing grace. The Bible says that, *"God resists the proud, but gives grace to the humble"* (James 4:6, Proverbs 4:34). God is drawn to weakness, *"My grace is sufficient for you: for my strength is made perfect in weakness"* (II Corinthians 12:9).

2. Repent—The second step in the pathway to victory over sin is to repent of all your ideas and ways to set yourself free. Secular ideas and self-help methods are all a reproach to Christ. You must admit that all your ways and man's ways are wrong. There is no 12-step program or method that can or will set you free. Ask God to forgive you for trying to go another way beside the way of the Cross. Admit to God that your ways have not worked, and only Christ and what He did on the Cross can set you free.

3. Accept God's Grace—You and I must accept His free grace for our problem with sin. Realize that you don't have to do some religious work to set yourself free; you must only receive the free gift of God's deliverance through faith in Christ. Paul said it so perfectly, *"I do not frustrate the grace of God: for if righteousness come by the law, then Christ is dead in vain"* (Galatians 2:21). Think about this for a moment. If you could set yourself free by your own willpower and keep the laws of God, then why did Jesus have to come and die a cruel death? If you couldn't live for God before you got saved, what makes you think you can do it now-except by the Lord's power?

4. Put Your Faith Exclusively in Christ and Him Crucified—Realize you were delivered two thousand years ago at the Cross. This is where the victory over sin was won. Whatever sin that has latched on to you must bow to the name of Jesus Christ. Every spirit of darkness and every sinful bent of your sin nature were defeated at the Cross. No matter how strong Satan's grip is on your life,

he must let go when your faith is placed completely in the shed blood of Christ.

The Children Of Israel

Remember when the children of Israel were delivered from Egyptian bondage? This is a physical example of our spiritual deliverance. No matter how many plagues God sent to Pharaoh, he still would not release the children of Israel. The terrible plagues of turning water to blood, an invasion of frogs, plagues of lice, swarms of flies, animals dying, breakout of boils, plagues of hail, infestation of locusts, and three days of complete darkness failed to break the grip that Pharaoh had on the Israelites. Pharaoh would not release the children of Israel from the bondage of slavery.

It wasn't until the tenth plague, death of the firstborn, that Pharaoh would let the children of Israel go. Death came over Egypt, smiting and killing every firstborn son in Egypt. Hebrew families placed the blood of a lamb over the doorpost of their homes, so when the death angel passed over and saw the blood, he would not kill their firstborn. This is a picture of our salvation and our victory over sin. Israel's deliverance from the bondage of slavery was through the blood of a lamb, which foreshadowed the shed blood of Jesus. The child of God today who is in slavery to sin's grip is delivered also by the blood of the Lamb.

Pharaoh was a type of Satan, and the children of Israel represent you and me. Pharaoh would not release his grip easily, and neither will Satan. But if the child of God will keep his faith completely in Christ and Him crucified, the devil must let go! Praise God! That is why Paul said, *"For I determined not to know any thing among you, save Jesus Christ, and him crucified"* (I Corinthians 2:2).

Satan must bow to the blood of Christ. This and only this is what releases his grip on humanity. As the old hymn writer wrote: *"Dear dying Lamb, Thy precious blood shall never lose its power, till all the ransomed Church of God be saved to sin no more."*

Human counseling that does not emphasize and place total dependence on the blood of Christ to set the prisoner free (no matter what the bondage is) is wrong counseling and will not set anyone free. Good Christian counseling will always take you to the Word of God and teach you the Message of the Cross. It will not add to the Cross. Sadly, some Christian counselors today are like the Judaizers of Paul's day. They believe in the Cross, but they don't believe the Cross is enough, so they add law unto grace.

But Paul said to the Galatian Christians who were believing the Judaizers, *"O foolish Galatians, who hath bewitched you,* (or fooled you into thinking) *that ye should not obey the truth, before whose eyes Jesus Christ hath been evidently set forth, crucified among you?"* (Galatians 3:1).

There are many false teachers today who have *"bewitched"* believers into thinking that the Cross of Christ is not enough. They teach that you must do something besides just believing in Christ and Him crucified. Paul went on to say in the next verse, *"Let me ask you this one question: Did you receive the Holy Spirit as a result of obeying the Law and doing its works, or was it by hearing* (the message of the Gospel) *and believing it?"* (Galatians 3:2).

Paul is pointing out to the Galatian believers that they should not move from believing the message of the Gospel, to trusting in their own abilities to keep the Law of God. He tells them to continue believing in the message of the Gospel, the message of Christ crucified and resurrected from the dead, as the only solution to sin.

Paul gives even more insight in the next verse when he asks, *"Are ye so foolish? having begun in the Spirit, are ye now made perfect by the flesh?"* (Galatians 3:3).

As a believer in Christ, you must not depend on or trust in the flesh. You cannot count on your own abilities, will power or performance to defeat the sin nature or the powers of hell. Become Cross-Eyed and see the Cross as your only solution to sin. From Genesis to Revelation, the Cross is the main theme of the Bible. The devil has done a good job of moving the modern Church away from the blood of Christ. We must come back to the Cross and trust what Jesus did there as the only solution to sin, the only way to live the victorious Christian life. God's grace is poured out on the believer who doesn't depend on works to earn his own victory, but looks to God's unmerited favor to give him victory.

When we truly receive the revelation of the Cross from the Lord, we will not want to emphasize anything else but the Cross. We will become single-minded, and we will not glory in anything else but the Cross of Christ (Galatians 6:14).

How The Holy Spirit Works

Let's talk about how the Holy Spirit works and how He gives us the victory that we seek. Christians misunderstand how to walk in the power of the Holy Spirit. The Bible's answer to overcoming the addictions of this world is by and through the power of the Holy Spirit. The Bible teaches us that it is not by human power but by the Spirit of God that we have victory (Zechariah 4:6).

Galatians 5:16 says, *"This I say then, Walk in the Spirit, and ye shall not fulfil the lust of the flesh."* This verse reveals the way to victory, walking in the power of the Holy Spirit. However, have you stopped to ask the question, *"How do I walk in the Spirit?"* Now that question is the most important question the believer will ever ask, and the answer is the most important one the believer could ever know.

The believer in Christ must understand how the Holy Spirit works, what moves Him, what grieves Him, what quenches His power, and what pleases Him. These truths of the Spirit are of utmost importance for the believer to live a victorious Christian life.

In Ephesians 1:17-19, Paul prays,

> *That the God of our Lord Jesus Christ, the Father of glory, may give unto you the spirit of wisdom and revelation in the knowledge of him: The eyes of your understanding being enlightened; that ye may know what is the hope of his calling, and what the riches of the glory of his inheritance in the saints, And what is the exceeding greatness of his power to us-ward who believe, according to the working of his mighty power.*

Cross-Eyed

Each believer in Christ must possess the wisdom, revelation and knowledge of the Lord to walk in victory. The devil will do whatever he can to veil from the believer these powerful truths of the Holy Spirit. The devil knows that the Holy Spirit is the power source for victory.

The Bible does not promise us that we won't be tempted by the flesh. To the contrary, the Bible warns us that we will be tempted. However, if we walk in the Spirit, the Bible does promise us that we will not carry out the lust of the flesh (Galatians 5:16). We have the power to turn away from sin because the power of the Holy Spirit is greater than the devil's power. The power of our sin nature is defeated by the presence of the divine nature living and working within us.

Romans 8:4 says, *"That the righteousness of the law might be fulfilled in us, who walk not after the flesh, but after the Spirit."* The Greek word for *"walk"* is *"peripateo,"* *"to order one's behavior or conduct."* The word *"after"* is *"kata,"* the root meaning for *"down,"* which suggests domination. A true Christian is one who orders his behavior in such a way that the Holy Spirit directs his or her life, which produces a righteous or sanctified life. The believer is not dominated by the evil nature.

Righteous living can only come by and through the Holy Spirit. Paul was relating in Romans 7 that he had tried to live by the law, and he only met failure. But when he received the revelation of the Cross, he began to understand how the Holy Spirit works. The Holy Spirit works totally within the parameters of our faith in Christ and Him crucified. When we understand this, we will begin to experience a righteous and holy life produced by the Spirit.

The Holy Spirit works by grace and not by works. Our salvation in Christ, which includes victory over sin, comes to us by the Spirit, and the Spirit works *"by grace through faith"* (Ephesians 2:8-9). Walking in the Spirit means that we order our behavior continuously in Christ (faith in Him and what He did on the Cross).

KEEP YOUR EYES ON JESUS

When a believer takes his eyes off Christ and what Christ has done for him at the Cross, he starts to live his Christian life by the law. The law of sin and death begins to dominate his life once again; and if he does not repent, that believer can slip back into a lifestyle that looks very much like the life he lived before he was saved. He will begin to live his Christian life in the flesh and not in the Spirit.

The flesh is our resident evil, sin nature. Our flesh is also our willpower and ability. The Bible tells us that our flesh is weak. Jesus said, *"Watch ye and pray, lest ye enter into temptation. The spirit truly is ready, but the flesh is weak"* (Mark 14:38).

Remember when Jesus called Peter out of the boat and Peter began to walk on the water to Jesus? It was when Peter took his eyes off Jesus to look at the waves around him that he began to sink (Matthew 14:30). The key to living the victorious Christian life is keeping our eyes on Jesus Christ and Him crucified.

If believers take their eyes off Jesus, they will begin to sink and come under condemnation (both by the devil and their consciences), because they have cut off the flow of the Spirit. One could say they have fallen from grace (Galatians 5:4), because they are not looking to grace and trusting in Christ and the Cross to give them victory. This is a miserable state, because there is no victory, only defeat and condemnation. It is a terrible feeling to be sinking and feeling as though you are drowning.

Paul knew this feeling when he penned the words, *"Oh wretched man that I am."* But once he understood how salvation worked (as he explained it in Romans 6), he experienced the victory of the Spirit working to conquer his sin nature. All of this was made possible by his faith in Christ and Him crucified.

The Holy Spirit began flowing freely in Paul's life because he shifted his dependence from *"I"* to Christ. Then the Holy Spirit began to be his emphasis, as we see by Paul's use of the word Spirit 16 times in Romans 8. The Holy Spirit produced a new energy in Paul's life, giving him the desire to do God's will. This is Romans 6 in a nutshell! The Holy Spirit works totally and completely within the parameters of our faith in Christ and what He has done for us through His death, burial, and resurrection (Romans 6:3-4).

THE THINGS OF THE SPIRIT

Our faith in Christ is very much connected to our mind. Faith comes from the heart (and is produced by the Spirit); it changes our mind (how we think). Romans 8:5 says, *"For they that are after the flesh do mind the things of the flesh; but they that are after the Spirit the things of the Spirit."*

People who are habitually sinning have their minds on the things that please their evil natures. This is the lifestyle of an unsaved person. But the true believer in Christ lives according to the Spirit and the things of the Spirit. Why? Because the divine nature is active and working.

Before I got saved, I had no desire to read the Bible, much less study it. However, the day I got saved, the Bible instantly became my favorite book. What I once couldn't understand now made all the sense in the world. Why? Because the divine nature had come in (II Peter 1:4), and the Holy Spirit was there to help teach me the Scriptures (John 14:26).

The mind of an unbeliever is on the things that please the flesh. However, the Christian has his mind on the things of the Spirit. Romans 8:6 says, *"For to be carnally minded is death; but to be spiritually minded is life and peace."*

The words *"carnally minded"* literally mean *"to have the mind of the flesh."* The flesh refers to the evil nature. The carnal mind is possessed and controlled or dominated by the evil sin nature. This again is a description of an unsaved person. This person is dead in his trespasses and sin, separated from God, and on his way to a final and everlasting state of death in eternity.[2]

The words *"spiritually minded"* describe a person whose mind is controlled or dominated by the Holy Spirit. A mind dominated by the Holy Spirit is going to produce life and peace, but a mind controlled by the evil nature will have no life and no peace but only misery, turmoil and despair. The mind of the believer should be on the things of the Spirit, not the things of the flesh.

What are the things of the Spirit and the things of the flesh? The things of the flesh are such things as pleasure, profit, personal satisfaction, worldly pursuits, selfish desires, etc. The things of the Spirit have to do with what pleases God. Righteousness, peace, holiness, the welfare of a soul, the concerns of eternity, the truths of the Word of God are the thoughts of one who is walking in the Spirit.

When walking in the Spirit, you are controlled by the Spirit; the things that the Spirit loves, you love. You'll find when you are truly walking in the Spirit that you experience a closeness to God. You will desire to study the Bible, your prayer life will increase in intensity, your passion for God and for souls will consume you. Walking in the Spirit is the most incredible experience you will ever find in this world. Even in the toughest trial of your entire life, the peace of God will bring you through it if you're walking in the Spirit.

QUENCHING THE SPIRIT

First Thessalonians 5:19 warns us to *"quench not the Spirit"*. The Greek word for *"quench"* is *"shennumi,"* which means *"to extinguish or to go out."* The Holy Spirit is like a fire burning in our lives. John said that Jesus would baptize us with the Holy Spirit and with fire (Luke 3:16). Just as water puts out literal fire, there are things that we do that put out the fire of the Holy Spirit.

What do you think quenches or puts out the fire of the Holy Spirit? Sin! The devil fools us and causes us to sin, and we don't even know we are sinning. Satan will constantly try to break the flow of the Spirit in the believer's life. How does he do that? He gets him to shift his faith from Christ and the Cross. If the devil can distract the believer into looking to other ways, methods, programs or selfish indulgences, he knows he has him. When the believer's eyes are taken off Christ and the Cross, the Spirit will be quenched in his life, and failure will soon follow.

Most believers know the obvious sins such as lust, jealousy, envy, unwholesome language, hatred, drunkenness, strife, etc.— the list goes on and on. But most believers do not see taking our eyes off the essence (the object) of our faith, Jesus Christ and Him crucified, as sin. But the Bible says, *"for whatsoever is not of faith is sin"* (Romans 14:23).

Any time the word *"faith"* is used in the New Testament, Paul or the writer is talking about *"The Faith"* – Jesus Christ and Him crucified, who He is and what He did. Paul defines the faith in Galatians 2:20,

> *I am crucified with Christ: nevertheless I live; yet not I, but Christ liveth in me: and the life which I now live in the flesh I live by the faith of the Son of God, who loved me, and gave himself for me.*

The modern Church often has its eyes on everything but the Cross of Christ, be it church growth, our purpose, prosperity, the gifts of the Spirit, prophetic utterance, etc. These things are important, but when they become more important than Christ and the Cross, we have lost the true object of our faith.

THE FIERY SERPENT

We read in the Book of Numbers that the Israelites had sinned by murmuring against God and placed themselves under His judgment (Numbers 21:6-9). God used poisonous snakes to punish them. The snakes were attacking the people, causing pain and even death. Moses interceded for the people to be healed, and God answered his prayer. Numbers 21:8 says, *"And the Lord said unto Moses, Make thee a fiery serpent, and set it upon a pole: and it shall come to pass, that every one that is bitten, when he looketh upon it, shall live."*

This is a type of Calvary. Christ died on the Cross, taking upon Himself the condemnation of sin. That is why God used the serpent on the pole. The serpent represented sin, and the pole represented the Cross. The Bible says, *"For he hath made him to be sin for us, who knew no sin; that we might be made the righteousness of God in him"* (II Corinthians 5:21).

God is showing, through the events in the Book of Numbers, that our eyes must always be on the sacrifice of Christ on the Cross. Our simple faith in Christ and Him crucified brings healing and life to our souls. Satan is ever trying to keep the believer's attention off the Cross. But as God told Moses so long ago, and Moses told the people, *"Look to the pole."* Numbers 21:9 says, *"And Moses made a serpent of brass, and put it upon a pole, and it came to pass, that if a serpent had bitten any man, when he beheld the serpent of brass, he lived."* Through His Word, God is telling us today, *"Look to the Cross."*

GRIEVING THE HOLY SPIRIT

Ephesians 4:30 says, *"And grieve not the holy Spirit of God, whereby ye are sealed unto the day of redemption."* The word *"grieve"* in the Greek language is *"lupeo,"* and means *"to distress, to be sad, to cause grief, to be in heaviness, or sorrow."* There are things (sins) that we believers do that cause the Holy Spirit to be sad, that go against the Spirit. This grief happens any time we are acting in the flesh or depending on the flesh for our strength.

When David sinned with Bathsheba by committing adultery, he grieved God. When he finally realized it, he confessed his sin and pleaded with God to not take His presence from him. David said, *"Cast me not away from thy presence; and take not thy holy spirit from me"* (Psalm 51:11).

In the Old Testament (before the Cross), the Holy Spirit would come upon believers, but the Holy Spirit would not come into a person's heart and abide. When the Day of Pentecost came, which was after Christ paid the price for sin on the Cross, the Holy Spirit began coming into the heart and life of every person who repented and placed his or her faith in Christ and Him crucified.

As believers in Christ today, we do not lose the Holy Spirit when we sin. But we do grieve the Spirit and thereby quench the flow of the Spirit. Anyone who has ever walked in the power of the Holy Spirit knows that sin causes the loss of that flow of the Spirit, breaking intimate fellowship with the Spirit; this is heartbreaking. Once we have known the intimacy of the Father brought by the Holy Spirit, we never want to lose that closeness. When we sin, we could say what David said in a little different way—*"Lord, please don't stop the flow of Your presence in my life, and please don't stop the Holy Spirit from working in my life."*

Cross-Eyed

Many today in the Body of Christ are not living in the presence and power of the Holy Spirit. This is tragic, because it is available to every Christian. An even greater tragedy is that most don't even know the Holy Spirit's power has been cut off.

SAMSON

Samson was a mighty man of strength. The Bible tells us that his strength was found in his hair. But the world then did not know the secret to Samson's great strength, just as the world today does not know or understand the strength of the Christian. When Delilah seduced Samson and persuaded him to give her the secret of his strength, she proceeded to strip him of his great power. When Samson lost his strength, the Bible says he didn't even know it had left him!

Judges 16:19-20 says,

> *And she made him sleep upon her knees; and she called for a man, and she caused him to shave off the seven locks of his head; and she began to afflict him, and his strength went from him. And she said, The Philistines be upon thee, Samson. And he awoke out of his sleep, and said, I will go out as at other times before, and shake myself. And he wist not that the Lord was departed from him.*

It wasn't until Samson really needed his strength that he found out that his power had left him. There are those today in the Body of Christ who have believed and followed a false way, not knowing that they have left the Cross, their first love. But when the tempter comes and they try to resist him, they find they have no strength or power to resist their sin nature; they find themselves falling into sin.

This is one of the reasons the divorce rate in the Church is the same as it is in the world. Many preachers today (thank God, not all) are not preaching the Cross, and therefore the power of the Spirit is gone. Even worse, those churches don't even know it's gone. When it comes to resisting the temptations of the world, they have no power, because the Spirit is quenched. They find themselves fighting their sin natures in the flesh.

Jesus told us expressly not to move our faith away from Him, but to stay right where we are, in Him. When we move our faith away from Christ and the Cross, we are left without the power of God's Spirit. As Jesus said, *"...for without me ye can do nothing"* (John 15:5).

What Moves The Holy Spirit

Did you ever stop to consider why the Holy Spirit came into your heart at the moment you were born again? What was it that caused the Spirit to come in?

It was faith and repentance working together that moved the Holy Spirit to come into your heart and life. Since that is what caused the Holy Spirit to initially come into your life, the same thing moves the Holy Spirit every moment and every day of your life.

The devil knows that the Holy Spirit moves in accordance to repentance and faith in Christ and what Christ did on the Cross. Therefore, the devil works his hardest at perverting the message of the Gospel to the lost, and he tries to move believers away from the Cross so that the Spirit will be quenched.

The Holy Spirit is the great gift of the New Covenant. He was sent to help us do what we couldn't do ourselves—defeat sin's power. Regarding the Holy Spirit, Jesus said, *"But the Comforter, which is the Holy Ghost, whom the Father will send in my name, he shall teach you all things, and bring all things to your remembrance, whatsoever I have said unto you"* (John 14:26).

The word *"Comforter"* in the Greek is *"parakletos,"* and means *"helper"* or *"one sent alongside to help"* or *"intercessor or consoler."* The Holy Spirit is sent to help us through the name of Jesus. We receive the Holy Spirit into our lives to help us every day to live for God through Jesus Christ. The Holy Spirit could not live inside a believer under the Old Covenant. Why? Because Christ had not yet atoned for sin. But now, under the New Covenant, we have an advocate, we have a Helper, we have a power source living within us, O Hallelujah!

Cross-Eyed

The believer must realize that the Holy Spirit does nothing separate from the Cross. I am going to say that again—the Holy Spirit does absolutely nothing apart from faith in Christ and what Christ did at the Cross.

THE BOOK OF ACTS

The student of God's Word can follow the Book of Acts and learn that God has a baptism of power that is available to every believer. The early Church received this power. *"And they were all filled with the Holy Ghost, and began to speak with other tongues, as the Spirit gave them utterance"* (Acts 2:4).

On the Day of Pentecost, the Lord poured out His Spirit and believers were baptized with power. Jesus told the disciples not to do anything before this power came on them, but to wait for it. *"And being assembled together with them, commanded them that they should not depart from Jerusalem, but wait for the promise of the Father, which, saith he, ye have heard of me"* (Acts 1:4). Jesus said to wait for *"the promise of the Father,"* which is the baptism of the Holy Spirit. Without the power of the Holy Spirit, we can do nothing that will truly glorify the Father.

Notice what Jesus said next. *"For John truly baptized with water; but ye shall be baptized with the Holy Ghost not many days hence"* (Acts 1:5). To be baptized with the Holy Ghost is to receive power from God. In Acts 1:8 Jesus said,

> *But ye shall receive power, after that the Holy Ghost is come upon you: and ye shall be witnesses unto me both in Jerusalem, and in all Judaea, and in Samaria, and unto the uttermost part of the earth.*

Every believer in Christ needs this baptism of power. A thorough study of the Book of Acts shows us repeatedly that the New Testament believers were receiving this baptism with the Holy Spirit. The devil will try to persuade the believer that it is not for today. However Peter (when speaking to the people on the Day of Pentecost, right after the Spirit fell) said these words,

> *Repent, and be baptized* (in water) *every one of you in the name of Jesus Christ for the remission of sins, and ye shall receive the gift*

of the Holy Ghost. For the promise is unto you, and to your children, and to all that are afar off, even as many as the Lord our God shall call.

Acts 2:38-39

Peter made it clear that the baptism of the Holy Ghost was not just for certain people during a certain time in history. To confirm this, we see a continuation in the Book of Acts of people receiving the baptism with the Holy Spirit (Acts 10:44, 11:15-16, 19:1-6).

The power of the Holy Spirit is essential for every believer. The Bible promises us that all those who are hungry and thirsty for God will be filled (Matthew 5:6). The most popular verse Christians give to the lost is John 3:16. But the verse that should be the most popular to be given to encourage other believers is Luke 3:16, *"John answered, saying unto them all, I indeed baptize you with water; but one mightier than I cometh, the latchet of whose shoes I am not worthy to unloose: he shall baptize you with the Holy Ghost and with fire."*

Even when the believer has been baptized with the Holy Spirit, that believer must still understand how the Holy Spirit works through faith in Christ and what Christ has done at the Cross. Without this, even though the power of the Holy Spirit is available to him, he will live in defeat. We see this in the life of the Apostle Paul. You must know how the Spirit works.

ANOTHER GOSPEL

There are many today who are not preaching the Cross, but another gospel. Paul was very strong in his warnings to those who were preaching another gospel. Galatians 1:8 says, *"But though we, or an angel from heaven, preach any other gospel unto you than that which we have preached unto you, let him be accursed* [excommunicated]."

You may say, *"Well, this particular preacher is not an evangelist, and that is why you don't hear him preaching on the Cross. He is a teacher of how to live for God."* Let me say something that may sound a little strong, but actually, in light of what Paul said (in Galatians 1:8), it is not. Any preacher, teacher, evangelist, pastor, prophet, apostle, or missionary that teaches from the Word of God and does not make the Cross of Christ the main emphasis in his teaching is preaching another gospel.

> *But I fear, lest by any means, as the serpent beguiled Eve through his subtilty, so your minds should be corrupted from the simplicity that is in Christ. For if he that cometh preacheth another Jesus, whom we have not preached, or if ye receive another spirit, which ye have not received, or another gospel, which ye have not accepted, ye might well bear with him.*

II Corinthians 11:3-4

Paul said these words which should awaken every believer to the fact that false teaching can be very subtle and clever. The word *"deceive"* in the Greek is *"exapatao,"* and means *"to seduce wholly."* Paul was afraid that the believers at Corinth would accept teaching that was false. He feared they would be deceived by the fact that the false teachers would use the same terminology or the same Christian lingo, but would distort the truth. So Paul warned them: just because somebody uses the name of Jesus does not make him a true teacher of the Word.

So beware: there will be teachers who use the name of Jesus and the Holy Spirit and call it the Gospel, but it will be another gospel. So how do you protect yourself from such deception? You must thoroughly understand the Word of God. Anyone or anything that takes your focus off Jesus Christ and Him crucified (the central truth of Christianity) is deception and is leading you away from the truth.

CHRISTIANS ARE A WORK IN PROGRESS

In this book I am not saying that you can live a spiritually perfect life, even though that is the goal—God's goal. This will not be fully achieved until we see Him in Heaven and He gives us an incorruptible body, free of the sin nature. However, as we learn how to walk in the Spirit, we should be failing God less and less. As when learning how to ride a horse, the rider should fall off the horse less and less. Walking in obedience with God is a process. The devil will occasionally succeed at getting the believer's eyes off Christ and the Cross. However, when we truly know how to walk in the Spirit, we may fall off the horse, but we will get right back up, brush ourselves off, and get right back on the horse. We'll be able to do this because we will know why we have fallen. The reason is we took our eyes off Christ and His finished work.

The key to Christian growth is adjusting our walk. A soldier in the military knows what his general expects. The Bible says in Romans 8:7-8,

> *Because the carnal mind is enmity against God: for it is not subject to the law of God, neither indeed can be. So then they that are in the flesh cannot please God.*

Another translation puts it, *"For the sinful nature is always hostile to God. It never did obey God's laws, and it never will. That's why those who are still under the control of their sinful nature can never please God"* (NLT).

The word *"subject"* is *"hupotass,"* a military term meaning *"to arrange in order under"*—under a commanding general, for instance. The carnal mind (or the fleshly mind) does not follow the mind of God but instead follows its own worldly lusts. That is why the carnal man cannot please God. But the true believer in Christ has the mind of Christ.

The Holy Spirit dwells in the life of every born-again believer, and His function is to give the believer victory over sin and to produce the fruit of the Spirit. The saved person should not be in the grip of the evil nature but in the sphere of the divine nature. Romans 8:10 says, *"And if Christ be in you, the body is dead because of sin; but the Spirit is life because of righteousness."*

The word *"body"* here is speaking of the believer's human body, which is dead due to the Fall. Therefore, the believer is helpless to overcome sin by his own willpower. All his efforts are futile. However, the Spirit can make him what he ought to be. Therefore, he must rely on the Holy Spirit to give him the victory. The Spirit will do that if his faith remains in Christ and Him crucified.

Romans 8:11 teaches,

> *But if the Spirit of him that raised up Jesus from the dead dwell in you, he that raised up Christ from the dead shall also quicken your mortal bodies by his Spirit that dwelleth in you.*

The words *"give life"* are *"zooporeo,"* which means to *"cause to live, make alive, give life."* This is speaking not only of a physical resurrection of the believer's body, but also it is speaking of the Holy Spirit giving us power in our mortal bodies to live a victorious Christian life. Here is a huge revelation—the same Spirit that raised Jesus from the dead is now living in the life of every believer. God has put such power in our lives!

Romans 8:12-13 says,

> *Therefore, brethren, we are debtors, not to the flesh, to live after the flesh. For if ye live after the flesh, ye shall die: but if ye through the Spirit do mortify the deeds of the body, ye shall live.*

Paul is saying the Christian should be constantly putting to death the deeds of the flesh. This is done by the Spirit working through our faith. Therefore we believers can take no credit or give any praise to the flesh; all of the praise for our victories over sin and death belongs to Christ. We are indebted to Him and what He has done on Calvary to redeem us.

When we believers know, believe, and trust in the important truths of Romans 6 through 8, we will experience incredible victory in our lives as we walk in the Spirit. However, if we are ignorant to the spiritual truths of Romans 6 through 8, then we will walk in defeat.

How To Know If You Are A True Believer

If a person lives under the dominion of the evil nature, sinning habitually, that person is unsaved, no matter what he or she may say. That person is on the way to final death in the lake of fire. But the person who, by the Holy Spirit, habitually puts to death the deeds of the flesh will live. That person is saved![3]

Christians are not perfect. We still falter and fail, however, it is the desire of our hearts not to sin. So when we do fail God, we hurt inside. We want to repent and restore our fellowship with God. The unbeliever does not care to restore fellowship with God because he never had fellowship with God to begin with.

How do you know if you are truly a believer in Christ? Here is a pretty good checklist:

1. Are you following the leading of the Holy Spirit in your life, or are you following your own fleshly lusts? Romans 8:14 says, *"For as many as are led by the Spirit of God, they are the sons of God."*

When the Holy Spirit is leading an individual, He will always lead them constantly to the Cross and away from sin. The Holy Spirit will lead you in the truth and will glorify Christ (John 16:13-14).

2. Do you have intimacy with God? The Holy Spirit will lead the child of God into a relationship with God the Father, for it is the desire of the Father to be close to His children. Romans 8:15 says, *"For ye have not received the spirit of bondage again to fear; but ye have received the Spirit of adoption, whereby we cry, Abba, Father."*

Paul had a close relationship with God and he cried, *"Abba, Father."* The word *"cry"* is *"krazo"* and it speaks of a loud cry of deep emotion. The word *"Abba"* is a Syrian term that Paul translates in the Greek *"the Father."* Jesus used this term in the Garden of Gethsemane in His prayer. The Holy Spirit enables the child of God to call God, Father. The Holy Spirit has adopted us into the family of God.

3. The Holy Spirit will give you witness within your heart that you are saved. *"The Spirit itself beareth witness with our spirit, that we are the children of God"* (Romans 8:16).

The Holy Spirit has energized our human spirit, and the change that He has brought into our lives proves that we are the children of God. If there has been no change in a person's life, then there is no witness within him that he is a child of God.

WHAT ARE THE BENEFITS OF THE CHRISTIAN LIFE?

Everything the believer receives from God was purchased at Calvary by Jesus Christ. Romans 8:17 says, *"And if children, then heirs; heirs of God, and joint-heirs with Christ; if so be that we suffer with him, that we may be also glorified together."*

Roman law made all children—including adopted ones—equal inheritors (Vincent). Jewish law gave a double portion to the eldest son. The suffering here is not referring to personal trial, but to suffering with Christ, which refers to the great price He paid at the Cross for us. He has been glorified, and we will be glorified one day also, because of the Cross.

No matter what problems or difficulties we go through in this world, they cannot compare to the future we have in Christ. *"For I reckon that the sufferings of this present time are not worthy to be compared with the glory which shall be revealed in us"* (Romans 8:18).

Our eternal future with Christ makes any suffering in this world bearable. Just keep looking to that day when we see Him! He is the finish line, so don't get tired and give up! The best is yet ahead! Glory to God!

Romans 8:19-21 says,

> For the earnest expectation of the creature waiteth for the manifestation of the sons of God. For the creature was made subject to vanity, not willingly, but by reason of him who hath subjected the same in hope, Because the creature itself also shall be delivered from the bondage of corruption into the glorious liberty of the children of God.

Verse 19 is referring to the coming resurrection of life. There is a great expectation in Heaven and on earth for the Resurrection Day. We were subjected to vanity by the fall of Adam, but there is a great day coming. The goal of the Christian's life is to know Him as closely as we can until that day when we see Him face-to-face.

The work of the Cross is what makes one holy and above reproach. You must realize that it has nothing to do with what we do—it's all about what Christ did on the Cross, and because of the Cross, the Spirit will move and operate in any person's heart and life whose mind is set on Him!

> *And you, that were sometime alienated and enemies in your mind by wicked works, yet now hath he reconciled in the body of his flesh through death, to present you holy and unblameable and unreproveable in his sight.*

> Colossians 1:21-22

Chapter Ten

It's A New Day!

Ever since Christ died on Calvary, it has been a new day. Jesus provided the way for a New Covenant to be born.

The Old Covenant's purpose was to put man on his face and let him see the depths of his sin. Man must see that he cannot meet God's holy standards. The law is a tutor to teach man that he needs Christ (Galatians 3:24).

The Old Covenant has done its job! It has shown us that we can't live without God's daily help. We are without strength and moral restraint. The evil nature is too powerful. The chains are too strong to break. We are too wicked in and of ourselves. We need help, big time!

Many Christians do not understand all that Christ did for them on the Cross. Many make the mistake of thinking that once they have the Holy Spirit, they are *"super Christians."* We have to be careful that the knowledge of who we are in Christ does not turn into spiritual pride. We must remember that when the Lord saved us, He didn't remove the sin nature—He simply stripped it of its power. If we don't depend on the Holy Spirit every moment, that sin nature will reappear.

The Holy Spirit is drawn to our weaknesses, not our strengths. Paul quoted Jesus in II Corinthians 12:9 when he said, *"And he said unto me, My grace is sufficient for thee: for my strength is made perfect in weakness."*

Here is a good prayer for the believer to pray continually:

Oh Lord, Your law has shown me that I am utterly helpless before You. I cannot in and of myself keep Your commands. I abandon all hope of getting free from sin's grip by my own strength. I acknowledge my dependence on Jesus and what He did on the Cross. I need Your Holy Spirit to help me live a holy life, and I know You will help me if my faith is completely in Christ. Thank You for setting me free at the Cross and not leaving me helpless, but sending Your Holy Spirit to live within me. In Jesus' name I pray. Amen.

Under the New Covenant, the battle over our sin nature is not our battle, but the battle belongs to the Lord. Romans 8:13 says,

For if ye live after the flesh, ye shall die: but if ye through the Spirit do mortify the deeds of the body, ye shall live.

The misdeeds of the body are the sins we commit. The problem is, many Christians try to kill the deeds of the body through their own flesh or willpower. When they do that, they are slipping back into the Old Covenant mindset.

THE CROSS

One of the most basic Christian doctrines is that the Cross of Jesus Christ renders any works of the flesh meaningless and without merit to God. Because of the Cross, no human goodness can ever contribute to a person's salvation (Wilkerson). Let me add to that - There is no human goodness that can ever contribute to a person's holiness, either. This is a work of God's grace as a result of the Cross and is accomplished through His Spirit. Glory to God!

The Cross in Jesus' day was a huge offense to the people who were steeped in legalism, trying to live for God by the law. Jesus' teaching was introducing a New Covenant, a new way of thinking. Instead of living by rituals and requirements, He taught that we must live by a relationship with God through the person of the Holy Spirit and to be totally dependent on God's power to fulfill the commandments of God.

The religious world of that day resisted this new teaching. Why? They were self-righteous people who liked taking the credit for their own righteousness, which was really no righteousness at all.

Paul also taught that, under the New Covenant, legalism is not the way to live.

Wherefore if ye be dead with Christ from the rudiments of the world, why, as though living in the world, are ye subject to ordinances, touch not; taste not; handle not,

Colossians 2:20-21

Paul was saying that anything that you think contributes to your salvation other than the blood of Christ is worthless (Wilkerson). The Cross offends the world (and the religious world especially) because the Cross says that all works of the flesh, legalistic rules and regulations, are worthless in the eyes of God.

The Christian statement that the Cross of Christ is the only way to salvation also offends most of the religious people in the world. Why? They are functioning under a law mindset, primarily looking at Moses and not Christ. This was also a problem in Jesus' day. John 9:28 says, *"Then they reviled him, and said, Thou art his disciple; but we are Moses' disciples."* As the old hymn writer wrote, *"Nothing in my hands I bring, simply to the Cross I cling."*

The death of Christ on the Cross signaled the end of the Old Covenant. Holiness became available through the Cross by the Spirit. Some people erroneously think that under the New Covenant (the covenant of grace), we are not under so strict a lifestyle. That assumption could not be further from the truth. Paul said, *"What shall we say then? Shall we continue in sin, that grace may abound? God forbid. How shall we, that are dead to sin, live any longer therein?"* (Romans 6:1-2). Another translation puts it, *"Well then, should we keep on sinning so that God can show us more and more kindness and forgiveness? Of course not! Since we have died to sin, how can we continue to live in it?"* (NLT).

The New Covenant is actually more restrictive because you now have God's Spirit living within your life, examining everything. Not only are your actions under the microscope, but so are your motives.

The New Covenant Unveiled

Once a believer understands the New Covenant, then he or she can learn the secret to total victory over sin. Death is the only way out of the Old Covenant and into the New. Faith in the flesh, the ability to earn salvation or sanctification, has to die. No more striving to believe. If I am to have faith—true faith, the faith of Christ—then He has to give it to me.[1]

When the children of Israel were ready to cross into the Promised Land, something tragic happened. Moses died! The courageous leader who had miraculously led them through the Red Sea, through the wilderness, and had gone to the mountaintop, visited with God and received the Ten Commandments, was now at the pivotal moment of finally arriving at the Promised Land. But he could only view it from a distance; he could not go into the land (Deuteronomy 34:1-5).

Why couldn't Moses go in? Why would God not allow him to cross over? Moses had made one big mistake as the leader of Israel. When the people were without water, God told Moses to speak to the rock (which was a type of Christ), and water would come out from it. But in anger over the people's rebellion and lack of faith, Moses didn't speak to the rock; he struck the rock. He disobeyed God. Numbers 20:11 says,

> *And Moses lifted up his hand, and with his rod he smote the rock twice: and the water came out abundantly, and the congregation drank, and their beasts also.*

The Lord was not pleased with Moses' outburst of anger.

> *And the Lord spake unto Moses and Aaron, Because ye believed me not, to sanctify me in the eyes of the children of Israel, therefore ye shall not bring this congregation into the land which I have given them.*

> Numbers 20:12

At first glance, it seems tremendously harsh for God to keep Moses from leading the Israelites into the Promised Land over one outburst of anger. I mean, up to this point he had been such an incredible leader!

The reason for the severe consequence for Moses' action is the rock's significance, what it represented. The rock was the spiritual

Rock of Israel, identified with the Messiah. When Moses struck the rock, it symbolized the crucifixion of Christ. Striking the rock twice meant crucifying Christ afresh. Also, Moses directly disobeyed a command from the Lord due to anger.

Unbelief is the basis for all sin. Notice the words God used to Moses, *"Because you did not believe in Me."* Moses' lack of belief and trust in the Lord caused his great failure.

Moses spent most of his 120 years either in preparation for or in the actual work of getting the children of Israel out of bondage and bringing them to the Promised Land. And now, at the pivotal moment of his journey, he was not permitted to see the work completed. God would use Joshua to lead the children of Israel into the Promised Land.

Moses, as representing the law, could not bring Israel into the Promised Land. He had to die, for he had failed to obey God's commands while under the law. God would only give the Israelites the Promised Land (which represents our salvation) if they had obeyed the law perfectly. Man, being a sinner, cannot give this perfect obedience.[2]

Joshua, Moses' successor, was a type of the Savior. *"Joshua"* is the Hebrew name for Jesus. Joshua represented grace operating in the power of the Holy Spirit. The law cannot give you victory; only grace by the Spirit through faith can set you free. If you live your Christian life under the law or the Old Covenant, you will be a servant to your sin nature, your Christian experience will be one of wandering in the wilderness. You will not be able to enter into all the promises God has for you.

If you live under grace and under the benefits of the New Covenant, which were purchased for you at the Cross, you will be a son in right relationship with God, experiencing the intimacy of the Father, and you will possess the land. Praise God!

Most Preachers Are Preaching The Law

Some preachers today will say with all sincerity that you need to fight sin and not allow your sins to ruin you. Some will preach hard against the lust of the flesh and tell you to turn away from those lusts. Some will tell you to bind the devil and run away from his temptations. However, they are asking you to do something that is humanly impossible. Even though they preach holiness, purity, and obedience, they do not tell you how! They will warn you of the consequences of sin, but they don't tell you how to obtain the power to obey and defeat the power of sin.

This was the central problem of the Old Covenant. It demanded perfect obedience, a wholehearted turning from sin, but the command was not accompanied by the indwelling power to obey. This is why God made a New Covenant with human kind.[3]

The truth is, the majority of Christians today struggle with sin. They love God and they don't want to grieve His Spirit; they just don't know how to live under the New Covenant. They have been taught an Old Covenant mindset—just try harder. The result is that they fail miserably, as all human flesh will fail. The struggling believer needs a revelation of the Cross. Upon receiving the revelation of the Cross, he will understand the New Covenant. Christ and the Cross are the New Covenant.

This book has been written to reveal what the Bible says regarding the New Covenant. However, not everyone who reads this book or hears the Message of the Cross preached gets the revelation. Why is that?

The psalmist tells us, *"The secret of the Lord is with them that fear him; and he will shew them his covenant"* (Psalm 25:14). Another translation puts it, *"The LORD confides in those who fear him; he makes his covenant known to them"* (NIV).

I believe the Lord will only release the revelation of the Cross (His covenant) to those who truly fear Him. The word *"fear"* means to *"show reverence."* Those who take God for granted will not learn the deeper truths of God. Those who respect, honor, and show great reverence for God will be the ones to whom He shows His secrets.

The Bible says in Jeremiah 29:12-13,

> *Then shall ye call upon me, and ye shall go and pray unto me, and I will hearken unto you. And ye shall seek me, and find me, when ye shall search for me with all your heart.*

The truths of God's Word—especially the truths of the New Covenant—are so precious to the Lord that He does not give them out to just anyone, but gives them to the person who is really seeking and searching to know Him in a deeper way. That is why Jesus spoke to the masses in parables. It was only to His disciples (the true followers of God), that He opened up with those truths and explained what He was really teaching. Matthew 13:10-11 says,

> *And the disciples came, and said unto him, Why speakest thou unto them in parables? He answered and said unto them, Because it is given unto you to know the mysteries of the kingdom of heaven, but to them it is not given.*

Jesus will only reveal the mysteries of the Kingdom to those who are really seeking after God. Precious jewels only belong in the hands of those who know how precious they really are and will appreciate them when received. The Bible says for us not to cast our pearls before swine (Matthew 7:6). It also says in Jeremiah 33:3, *"Call unto me, and I will answer thee, and show thee great and mighty things, which thou knowest not."*

I truly believe most revelation from God only comes in times of brokenness. It is through brokenness that we are brought to a point of humility, desperation and need for God. Only when we cry out to God with our whole heart will He open up the secrets of victory over the obstacles we are facing.

God keeps the mysteries of the Kingdom hidden from the world that does not seek Him. Matthew 13:13 says,

> *Therefore speak I to them in parables: because they seeing see not; and hearing they hear not, neither do they understand.*

If you will take the truths of the Bible and seek God, His secrets will be revealed to you in ways you have never known were possible.

The Church Needs A Revelation

God gave a mighty revelation to the prophet Ezekiel. It is found in Ezekiel 37: 1-2, which says,

> *The hand of the Lord was upon me, and carried me out in the spirit of the Lord, and set me down in the midst of the valley which was full of bones, And caused me to pass by them round about: and, behold, there were very many in the open valley; and, lo, they were very dry.*

The vision that God gave Ezekiel specifically deals with Israel. The valley of dry bones that Ezekiel saw illustrates Israel's lack of spirituality. Israel's situation today is due to its refusal to accept Jesus as its Messiah. Israel ultimately will be restored at the second coming of Christ.

However, this vision also contains spiritual truths for the Church. Ezekiel was seeing in the Spirit—the way God sees. He saw a spiritually dead people. Any person, Christian or non-Christian, who does not understand the New Covenant—what Christ did at the Cross—will live in a valley of dry bones (dead religion).

Right now there are millions of people who believe in Jesus, but they are living in the valley of dry bones. You may be living in that valley right now, of depression, anxiety, mental sickness, or where the lust of the flesh controls your life. It could be a valley of any kind of sinful vices, where you are not experiencing the fire for the Lord in your heart.

The lack of fire in the believer's life is a prevalent problem in the Church today. Many Christians' lives look like valleys filled with dry bones. Most of the modern Church has either denied, ignored, or rejected the Holy Spirit, and accordingly, has moved away from the Cross. A segment of the Church emphasizes the Holy Spirit or the anointing of the Spirit, but because they have left the Cross, they are only chasing strange spirits that are not the Holy Spirit.

Most of the traditional denominations are trying to preach the Cross (if they are preaching the Cross at all) without the Holy Spirit. Most of the pentecostals and charismatics are trying to preach the Holy Spirit without the Cross. Why? We have left our first love and turned to idols. We have left the simplicity of Christ and turned our attention to self improvement. Whatever sells or builds bigger churches is the order of the day. Most of the modern Church has lost its way because it has taken its eyes off Jesus and the blood that was shed for the sins of the world.

Ask yourself: How many sermons have you heard about the Cross in the past year? How many about sin, righteousness and judgment? If the Holy Spirit is alive and well in the Church, then most Sundays, if not every Sunday, you will hear the preacher talking about the Cross. There will be conviction of sin, righteousness and judgment because this is what the Holy Spirit came to do, according to John 16:8, which reads,

And when he is come, he will reprove the world of sin, and of righteousness, and of judgment.

A later verse says,

Howbeit when he, the Spirit of truth, is come, he will guide you into all truth: for he shall not speak of himself; but whatsoever he shall hear, that shall he speak: and he will shew you things to come. He shall glorify me: for he shall receive of mine, and shall shew it unto you.

John 16:13-14

The role of the Holy Spirit is to regenerate the heart of man and to live inside the believer (John 3:3). He comes to glorify Jesus Christ (John 16:14) in the life of every believer. The Holy Spirit reveals truth to the believer (John 14:16-17,26; 16:13; Isaiah 11:6). He will reprove the believer of sin and correct his life (John 16:8-11).

It is also the function of the Holy Spirit to empower believers to be bold witnesses for Christ (Acts 1:8). He will work miracles through the believers (I Corinthians 12:11), and He anoints the believers for service (Luke 4:18-19).

One of the Holy Spirit's most important functions in the believer's life is to give the believer victory over sin (Romans 8:2,

Galatians 5:16). That is why *"Cross-Eyed"* has been written, to explain this all-important truth.

To determine if the Holy Spirit is alive and functioning in your life or in your Church, try this examination.

Is there a strong desire in your life to glorify Jesus Christ and the works of Christ? Are you more concentrated on self and on what Christ can do for you rather than glorifying Him? Is there continual truth from God's Word being revealed to you? Do you have a hunger for God's Word? Is there a constant flow of conviction of sin and repentance going on in your life? Have you been filled with the Holy Spirit? Is there a continual boldness in you to share Christ with a lost world? Are you witnessing God performing miracles in your life and using you in the gifts of the Spirit that are recorded in I Corinthians 12:7-11? Are you walking in victory over sin and living the victorious Christian life?

If your eyes are fixed on Jesus Christ and Him crucified, you will see the moving and operation of the Holy Spirit. When you are living under grace (Ephesians 2:8-9, Romans 6:14), you will notice that all you want to do is worship and glorify Jesus Christ and what He has done to redeem you. If Jesus is the focus of all your worship, that is a good indication the Holy Spirit is alive and active in your life.

LITTLE JESUS, LITTLE POWER; NO JESUS, NO POWER

Many of our songs and sermons are not focused on Jesus, the blood, the Cross, etc. Today there is more emphasis on self and the *"Blessing,"* be it prosperity, anointing, the increase, the *"hundred fold blessing,"* The Church is moving away from the old rugged Cross.

Even the contemporary Christian music industry has shifted away from using the name of Jesus in their songs. Record companies are telling the artists it's okay to use *"God,"* but not the name of Jesus because that name is offensive to many people and you will not sell as many albums. What a reproach this is in the eyes of God.

Has the Church lost its bold witness? I am afraid we have. We have bought the lie that, if we water down the Gospel a little bit, we will reach more people. You may reach more people, but you won't reach them for Jesus; you will just reach them to increase your church membership. The more we water down the Gospel, the more the Holy Spirit will pull back. The more the Holy Spirit moves back, the less of Jesus we will have. The less of Jesus we have, the less we will see the Holy Spirit's power at work.

The Dry Bones Can Live!

Ezekiel saw that the bones were dry, and the Lord asked, *"Can these bones live?"* Now, there is only one way to cure spiritual dryness. Look at the words of Jesus in Luke 4:18-19,

> *The Spirit of the Lord is upon me, because he hath anointed me to preach the gospel to the poor; he hath sent me to heal the brokenhearted, to preach deliverance to the captives, and recovering of sight to the blind, to set at liberty them that are bruised, to preach the acceptable year of the Lord.*

Jesus declared just what it takes to set the captives free. To resurrect dry bones, preach the Message of the Cross under the anointing of the Spirit.

The Lord told Ezekiel, *"Thus saith the Lord God unto these bones; Behold, I will cause breath to enter into you, and ye shall live"* (Ezekiel 37:5). This verse is a type of our salvation. At the moment a person repents of his sin and places his faith in Christ and what Christ did at the Cross to save him, then the Spirit of God breathes into his soul and brings life to his dry bones. The dry bones then begin to shake and rattle and come together. The good news is that a life that is broken in pieces and shows no sign of life can live! God can perform a miracle and resurrect that which is dead.

Prophesy To This Generation

To see the breath of God placed into the dry bones, God told Ezekiel to prophesy. *"So I prophesied as I was commanded: and as I prophesied, there was a noise, and behold a shaking, and the bones came together, bone to his bone"* (Ezekiel 37:7). Verse 9 goes on to say,

Cross-Eyed

> *Then said he unto me, Prophesy unto the wind, prophesy, son of man, and say to the wind, Thus saith the Lord God; Come from the four winds, O breath, and breathe upon these slain, that they may live.*

The word *"prophesy"* in the Greek is *"naba,"* which means *"to speak* (or sing) *by inspiration."* If we want to see revival in America, we must prophesy (speak or preach) over this generation through the inspiration of the Holy Spirit.

The dry bones represented dead and lifeless people. God told the prophet to prophesy to them so they would live. We can preach to a dead congregation all we want about turning from sin and living holy lives, but until we open to them the truths of the New Covenant and see a moving of the Holy Spirit, we are not going to see any life in those dry bones.

THE NEW COVENANT

If you as a believer will fully understand and live under the New Covenant, which is Christ and Him crucified, then and only then will you experience the life of the Spirit. On the night before He went to the Cross, when serving the disciples at the last supper, Jesus said,

> *This is my body which is given for you: do this in remembrance of me. Likewise also the cup after supper, saying, This cup is the new testament in my blood, which is shed for you.*

> Luke 22:19-20

So Jesus established the New Testament or New Covenant for us on the Cross. It is by grace through faith in what Jesus did on the Cross that the repentant believer obtains all the benefits of the New Covenant.

The Spirit brings the benefits of the New Covenant into the dry, lifeless bones of a person. This will bring new life to the world and revive the believer. Ezekiel saw a great vision of the future of Israel when at the second coming of Christ, He will restore them. His vision is for us today who understand the New Covenant and

134

place our faith properly in it. It will cause a revival of unexpected proportions. Ezekiel 37:10 finishes by saying,

So I prophesied as he commanded me, and the breath came into them, and they lived, and stood up upon their feet, an exceeding great army.

Chapter Eleven

Becoming Cross-Eyed

When the Holy Spirit opens your eyes and gives you the revelation of the Cross, you will begin to see the Cross everywhere in Scripture. From Genesis to Revelation, the Cross can be found in every portion of the Bible.

In the life of Abraham, we see that he often built altars, in fact, he was called an altar builder. The altar was where the sacrifice was placed and the blood of innocent animals was poured out. The altar of sacrifice in the Old Testament was a type of Calvary.

With the perspective of the altar being a type of the Cross, you can learn incredible truths from the Old Testament. For example, the Bible speaks of a river that will run down the main street of the New Jerusalem during the thousand-year reign of Christ (see Ezekiel 47:1-12).

> *Afterward he brought me again unto the door of the house; and, behold, waters issued out from under the threshold of the house eastward: for the forefront of the house stood toward the east, and the waters came down from under from the right side of the house, at the south side of the altar.*

Ezekiel 47:1

The source of this life-giving river, which brings healing to all, comes from the altar. Remember, an altar is a type of Calvary—if you want the river of God to flow in your church or in your youth ministry or in your own personal life, then you must understand that the river of God (the Holy Spirit) flows from the Cross. Jesus Christ is the source, and the Cross is the means.

Every true revival comes when the people are directed back to the Cross. Reformist Martin Luther led the great Protestant Reformation when he received a revelation from the Word of

God that shook the Catholic world and started the Protestant denomination. It was the Message of the Cross, proclaimed by the scripture that says the *"just shall live by faith."* That message is what sets people free from their religious bondages.

Martin Luther's message revolutionized the Christian world— the whole world, for that matter. It was a message of simple faith, not works. He stood on the Word and proclaimed that it was what Christ did on the Cross that makes you worthy, and believing in that fact saves and delivers you.

Throughout history, when men and women received the revelation of the Cross, awakening and revival followed. Martin Luther once said, *"If you want to see the reformation, look at the Cross; and if you look at the Cross, you will see the reformation."*

THE RIVER FLOWS FROM THE CROSS

When Jesus died, the Roman soldier came to the Cross, where Jesus was hanging lifeless. The soldier, making sure Jesus was dead, pierced Jesus' side with his spear. The Bible says that blood and water came out (John 19:34). The shedding of blood was for the remission of sins. The water flowed out when the soldier pierced Jesus' heart and broke the water sack that surrounded the heart. Water in scripture is used at times as a symbol of the Word of God and the Holy Spirit.

Jesus said that rivers of living water would flow out of the bellies of those who believe in Him (John 7:37-39). The river of God is brought into the heart of everyone who will believe in Jesus Christ and Him crucified. The Holy Spirit is that river!

In Revelation 22:1-3, we see the river that flows down the main street of heaven. It is a pure river, and it is a symbol of the Holy Spirit. On both sides of the street are the trees of life, and the fruit of these trees is for the healing of the nations. When we take a careful look, we see that the river is flowing from the throne of God. We know that Revelation 5:11-13 tells us that all of Heaven worships the One who sits on the throne and the slain Lamb of God. The river of God will flow in the heart of every believer who has his whole life centered on God the Father and Jesus Christ, the

Lamb who was slain at the Cross to set us free. The throne is the source of the river.

A PROPER CONFESSION

Jesus asked the disciples,

> *"Who do men say that I, the Son of Man, am?" They said, "Some say that you are John the Baptist, some say you are Elijah or Jeremiah or one of the prophets." But when Jesus said, "But who do you say that I am?" Peter said, "You are the Christ, the Son of the living God"*

Matthew 16:13-16.

Peter's confession was the one that Jesus was looking for. Peter acknowledged the Gospel truth that Jesus Christ was (and is) the Messiah, the Savior of the world. Peter's confession is the Gospel truth on which the whole Church was founded. Jesus said, *"Upon this rock, I will build My Church."* He was saying that the whole Church is built on the foundation of the Rock, which is Christ.

THE CROSS IS EVERYTHING

In the Book of Exodus we learn that the Old Testament Tabernacle, which God designed, was laid out in the shape of a cross. The Ark of the Covenant in the Holy of Holies was where the glory of God dwelled. The glory of God would hover over the Mercy Seat, which is also a type of the Cross (Exodus 25:17-18).

In Leviticus, the offerings were a type of Christ on the Cross (Leviticus, chapters 1-7). If you understand the Book of Leviticus, you will have a far better understanding of what Jesus accomplished on the Cross. In Leviticus, you will see the hatred that God has for sin, the wrath of God against sin, and the love that God has for the sinner.

The terrible suffering and pain that God brought about through the ritual sacrifices of the millions of innocent animals was a foreshadowing of the coming sacrifice that Jesus would make on the Cross. In studying the Levitical sacrifice, one will come to appreciate God's amazing grace, which was exhibited at the Cross of Calvary. The key to the sacrificial offerings in the Book of

Leviticus is that the sacrifice had to be without blemish—a type of the perfect Lamb of God, who was without sin.

If you were living in the Old Testament days, you would be responsible for bringing your animal sacrifice to the brazen altar to be slain. This would be your best animal—without spot or wrinkle. You would stand in a line of sinners, all holding their animals as well. As you moved closer to the altar, you would see the Levitical priests using their knives to slash the throat of the innocent animals and the hot blood of the doomed animals would flow into a basin. You would get a firsthand look at the terrible consequence of sin. You would sense the awful pain and suffering resulting from disobeying God.

You would watch as the priests washed the blood off their feet and hands at the brazen laver. You would hear the bellowing screams of the animals as their throats were slit, and you would be sickened by the scents of blood, oil, and black smoke from the burning flesh of the animal. All of this was a part of the sacrifice. This was no church picnic. By understanding the Levitical offering instituted by God, you will learn how terrible sin is in the eyes of a holy God. The cost of sin is great, for the Bible says that the wages of sin is death (Romans 6:23). We see that in God's economy, someone has to pay the price for sin.

Every man has a choice: he can receive the sacrifice of Christ as the atonement for his sin, or he can reject it. But no one gets away with sin. God knows all and sees all, and He is keeping a record of our sins. The Bible says that not one thing is missed by the eyes of God (Revelation 20:12). The miserable fact is that billions of people have died choosing not to place their faith in the slain Lamb of God. Could there be anything more horrifying or utterly disastrous than this in life? I say not!

CALVARY WAS A HORRIBLE SIGHT

The scene at Calvary was so horrible that even God could not look upon it. God darkened the skies over Calvary on the day when Jesus hung on the Cross. He was beaten, His beard was plucked from His face, and His back was cut into pieces from the scourging. He walked in a weakened state up Mount Calvary to the top of Golgotha *("the place of the skull")*. There was a trail of bloody footprints leading up to the hill, the footprints of a King!

Mount Calvary, on that day so long ago, was so horrible and so ghastly that God attempted to hide it. Darkness fell over Jerusalem the last three hours that Jesus was on the Cross.

When we think of the incredible sacrifice that was made for us at the Cross, we should be motivated to keep the Message of the Cross more important than anything else in our church. The Cross is not one issue, or just one of the doctrines of the faith, or something that was just for our salvation, something we move away from after we get saved. Such thinking is disrespectful and is an utterly reproachable stench in the nostrils of Almighty God.

The Cross is the central act of human history. The life and death of Christ split time in half, BC to AD. The Cross and what Jesus did there should be the center of all our preaching, teaching, and worship. It should be the meditation of our hearts for our entire lives, all the way to glory. Then, when we get to glory, we will really understand the revelation of the Cross fully. It will be the only reason why we are even in heaven at all. We will thank God for the Cross for all eternity!

MORE CONVINCING PROOF

In Joshua, chapter 2, there is a story of a harlot by the name of Rahab. She demonstrated faith in God and protected the Israelite spies. Israel's army spared her life and her home when they invaded Jericho. The army destroyed everything except her family and friends that were gathered in her home. Their lives were spared as a reward for her act of faith.

The spies had told her to place a scarlet red cord outside her window so, when the army invaded the city, they would not destroy that house. The scarlet cord represents the blood of Christ. It is only the blood that can protect you from the judgment of sin. No matter if you are a prostitute, drug addict, drunk, or even a murderer—if you will repent and place your faith in Christ and His shed blood on the Cross, you will be saved from the coming destruction that will occur on the Day of Judgment. Jesus Christ is the Redeemer and His shed blood is the red cord of redemption.

In I Kings 18, Elijah was fed up with all the false prophets of his day and how they were leading the people astray. So Elijah told all the false prophets to meet him on the mountain at high noon. He built an altar and dug a trench around the altar and told them to fill it with water. He then split a bull and put it on the altar.

Elijah then directed the 450 prophets of Baal to call on their god and ask their god to send down the fire and burn up the sacrifice. They cried out, but there was no response. Elijah began to mock them and told them that maybe their god was busy or on a vacation.

Then Elijah called on his God, and his cry brought down the fire of God onto the altar and burned up the sacrifice. Then all the people fell on their faces and shouted *"The Lord, He is God! The Lord, He is God!"* They then proceeded to destroy all 450 of the false prophets.

This whole scene is a type of Calvary. The fire of God represents the judgment of God. Jesus was the perfect sacrifice, and the fire of God's judgment fell on Him, just as it fell on the bullock that day on Mount Carmel. He took the punishment of sin for the entire world.

DAVID HAD A REVELATION OF THE CROSS

In Psalms, chapter 22, King David got a revelation of the Cross and became an example of Grace in the Old Testament.

My God, my God, why hast thou forsaken me? why art thou so far from helping me, and from the words of my roaring?

Psalm 22:1

Psalm 22 gives a description of Christ on the Cross that David saw long before it actually happened. God gave him a prophetic look into the future. David looked ahead to the Cross and believed. Today we look back to the Cross and believe. This belief brought him under Grace and not Law. The Lord had shown David, through a vision, Jesus Christ and Him crucified. Because of his faith in what he saw, David was acting as a New Covenant believer in the Old Testament. That is why he had no veil in his tabernacle. David's tabernacle was a place of incredible worship, evidenced by the songs that are recorded in the Book of Psalms. David's tabernacle was a place of freedom because of his *"revelation of the Cross."* It was open 24 hours a day, seven days a week.

BECOMING CROSS-EYED

When God begins to give a person the revelation of the Cross, that person will see the Cross everywhere in Scripture. In Daniel, the lion can't attack Daniel, which is a type of the defeat of Satan at the Cross.

In Hosea, God tells Hosea to marry a prostitute and to forgive her of her past. This is an example of God's forgiveness toward us—again, all brought about by Christ's death on the Cross (Hosea 2-3).

In Joel, the ministers weep continually before the altar. This is speaking of the brazen altar, where the sacrifices were offered, which is a type of Calvary (Joel 1:13).

In Amos, the prophet brings the message of judgment on the people. This is a form of the judgment that the whole world faces because of sin and, today, is only avoided by believing in what Christ did on the Cross for you.

In Obadiah, the prophet proclaims judgment on Edom but declares that there is a Savior that will come to save them from their sins (Obadiah 1:21).

Jonah was a man who was swallowed by the *"fish"* and was in its belly for three days before it spat him out, which was a type of the death, burial, and resurrection of Jesus (Jonah 1:17, Matthew 12:40).

In the Book of Habakkuk, the prophet speaks about writing down the vision. He says the vision is yet for the appointed time and says, though it tarries, wait for it—it will not delay. The vision the prophet is speaking about is Christ dying on the Cross to save us from our sins. He then declares that the *"just shall live by faith."*

The prophet understood grace and mercy as he wrote that the only way a man can be justified is by faith in the vision, and that vision is Christ and Him crucified (Habakkuk 2:2-3).

In Malachi, the prophet speaks of the people offering a blemished sacrifice. They were not giving the Lord their best animal as a sacrifice for their sins and God would not accept it. The only sacrifice that God will accept is a perfect sacrifice, and the only perfect sacrifice is Jesus Christ and His death on the Cross.

The Lord will not accept all of our good works as a payment for our sins. Millions of people are trying to gain God's acceptance by their own acts of righteousness (which are only filthy rags in the eyes of God). But these things will not earn us one ounce of favor with God. They are all blemished or imperfect works. It is only faith in Christ and what Christ has done that will bring the favor of God into our lives, because the only sacrifice that God will accept is a perfect one.

THE NEW TESTAMENT

In all four Gospels and the Book of Acts, the central message is Jesus Christ and Him crucified, risen from the dead. Everything points to that act in human history. It is the very reason Jesus came to this earth; He was born to die.

In the Book of Romans, Paul writes that it is only through the Cross that the believer can live a victorious Christian life. In the Book of Romans we learn how our salvation works. We learn that His blood justifies us and that our faith saves us, not our works (Romans 5:1). Also, it is our faith in the finished work of Christ that delivers us from the dominion of sin (Romans 6:14).

In I Corinthians 1:18, Paul tells the church that the Message of the Cross holds the power of God, and in 1:23 that the mission of the Church is to preach the Message of Christ and Him crucified. Paul told the Church that this Message of the Cross was all he determined to know—that Christ and Him crucified is the most important truth from which all other truths stem (1 Corinthians 2:2).

In II Corinthians 5:17, Paul tells us the believer is a new creature because of what Christ did on the Cross. Paul also outlines the spiritual gifts for the Church in this book, but the gifts are always to be kept in the right perspective—love is most important. The Bible says that there is no greater love than this, that one has laid down his life for his friends (John 15:13). This speaks of what Jesus did on the Cross for us.

In Galatians, Paul warns of preaching any other Gospel than the true Gospel. He says there is only one Gospel to preach; that is the Gospel of Grace. He states strongly that anyone who preaches another Gospel, other than the Gospel that he preached, which was Christ and Him crucified, was to be excommunicated from the Church (Galatians 1:8). Paul said he will only glory or boast in the Cross of Christ (Galatians 6:14). It was his everything, and it should be the believer's everything. Paul was a fanatic for the Cross and so should every believer be. Without the Cross, we would die in our sins and be lost forever and ever in hell.

In Ephesians 1:7, the Word of God declares that we have redemption through the blood that was shed on the Cross. Ephesians also teaches that it is through Jesus' death on the Cross that the wall of separation, which was between God and us, has been torn down (Ephesians 2:1-16).

In Philippians, Paul shared his desire to know the power of the resurrection of Jesus Christ. He wanted to fellowship in Jesus' sufferings, and he wanted to be conformed to His death on the Cross (Philippians 3:10). Paul was consumed with love for His Savior because of what He did for him on the Cross.

Colossians 2:14-15 speaks of how Christ has spoiled principalities and powers and made a public spectacle of the devil and all his demons. All of this was done on Calvary!

In I Thessalonians 1:5, the Word of God tells us that the Gospel of Christ (Christ's death, burial and resurrection) did not come in Word only but also in power. This book predicts that Jesus is coming back for His Bride (His Church).

Cross-Eyed

Second Thessalonians 1:8 tells us that there is a great punishment awaiting those who don't know God or who don't obey the Gospel of Jesus Christ. It also speaks of a great falling away just before the second coming of Jesus Christ (II Thessalonians 2:3). When we take our eyes off Christ and what He has done for us at the Cross, there will always be a falling away. That is why the devil works so hard to get the believer's attention away from the Cross.

In I and II Timothy, we are told to *"fight the good fight of faith"* (I Timothy 1:18-19 and II Timothy 6:12). I'd like to point out that the Bible never tells us to fight sin. We don't have to fight sin because someone already has defeated sin. Jesus Christ defeated sin at Calvary! But what we are to fight is the good fight of faith. Satan is always trying to destroy our faith or move our faith away from the Cross, the finished work of Christ. We must stay diligent in God's Word and keep our eyes fixed on Jesus and His blood that was shed for us.

In II Timothy, we are told that Christ abolished death and brought life to this old sinful world. How did He do this? He did it by His death and resurrection (II Timothy 1:10).

In Titus, Paul says that false teachers must be stopped (Titus 1:10). These false teachers were trying to mix the law and grace together for salvation. There must be no mixture of works and grace. We are saved by God's grace, which was done by Him sending His Son to die for us. Our righteousness before God comes totally and completely underserved. It comes by faith and faith alone (Titus 3:5).

In the Book of Philemon, we learn that all good things in us are from Christ, and the way that Christ can come into our hearts is upon our faith in what He did for us on the Cross (Philemon 1:6).

Hebrews is one of the most incredible books in the Bible. It is all about the Cross. A complete study of the Book of Hebrews will give the believer a clearer understanding of the New Covenant, which is all about the blood that Jesus shed for the remission of sins.

In James, saving faith is described as a faith that will produce a change in one's life. Just to say you believe but not change is the same as demons saying they believe (which they do), but they are not saved (James 2:19). The Books of Peter, John, and Jude all point to Christ and what He did on the Cross.

THE FOCUS OF HEAVEN

When you study the Book of Revelation, you find that Christ is referred to as the *"Lamb"* twenty-five times. You will notice that the scripture doesn't say the Lamb that was resurrected, but it says the *"Lamb that was slain"* Does that mean the resurrection isn't important? No, without the resurrection of Christ we are all still lost in our sins. The resurrection validates the Cross and shows us that God has accepted the sacrifice of Christ. Actually one should never separate the Cross and resurrection. They go together. However, the reason the scriptures emphasize the slain Lamb of God is that it was at the Cross where the sin debt was paid in full.

When the Lord opens the eyes of the believer to the revelation of the Cross, that person will begin to see the Cross everywhere in scripture. You will not be able to pick up your Bible and not see it. It is the Cross, the Cross, the Cross that has set you free. If only the Church would see it and return to the old rugged Cross as its focus, we would see a sweeping revival all across the world.

There is nothing else that has occurred in human history that can set man free. Christ's blood was shed on the tree to save this old world. For sinful man, there is nothing even remotely close to the importance of the Cross. It is the only way to heaven!

So, it's time for the Church of Jesus Christ to become *"Cross-Eyed."*

Chapter Twelve

"If You Build It, He Will Come"

It was Easter week 1999, and I was seeking the Lord in prayer and fasting. I was searching for direction for our ministry, Joshua Revolution. In 1993, we had first begun producing an annual youth conference at Christmas time in Niagara Falls. The Lord had greatly blessed this event, and we were getting the impression that we were to begin taking the conference to other cities across America.

But I could not venture into other cities without first getting a clear call from the Lord to do so. On Good Friday 1999, my wife Kathy and I went to our church service and then went to dinner. It was my intention to break a week-long fast. I had not heard a thing from the Lord in my time of prayer and study of the Word regarding the youth conference, so in my mind it was not the Lord's will for us to venture out to other cities at that time.

When the waitress served my meal, I heard a voice in my heart say, *"Don't eat."* To my wife's surprise, I asked the waitress to wrap my meal to go. I sensed the Lord didn't want me to break the fast yet, and that He had something He wanted to reveal to me.

I went home with every intention to seek the Lord. But when I got home, our four-year-old son Drew needed my attention. After spending time with him, I remember feeling very tired and saying to the Lord, *"Lord, I am so tired. I am going to go to bed and get up in the morning and seek You."*

I then turned on the TV (that always seems to put me to sleep). I flipped through the channels until I came to a familiar movie, *Field of Dreams.* The main character Ray Kinsella hears a voice while working in his cornfield. I remembered the voice saying, *"If you build it, they will come,"* but actually that was not quite right. What the voice actually says is, *"If you build it, he will come."*

When I heard that line, it was as if the Spirit of God invaded my living room. I had been asking the Lord in prayer all week if we should build the conference in other cities across America. I knew the Lord was giving me the answer to my prayers, but I had to be sure! I mean, I couldn't let the voice of Shoeless Joe be my call. So I asked the Lord, *"Build what, Lord?"* He said very clearly, *"I want you to build the Niagara conference in cities across America, and I want you to build My church."* From that night until now, we have attempted to fulfill that call.

BUILDING GOD'S CHURCH

A short time after receiving this Word from the Lord, I learned about the book *God's Favorite House: If You Build it, He Will Come.* Now, how long do you think it took me to go out and get a copy of this book? Even though I had never heard of the author, Tommy Tenney, the title intrigued me. I felt as though when I read that book, God would give me greater revelation of how to build His church.

Brother Tenney's writings would bring me closer in my quest. He wrote,

"God is looking for a church that has learned how to build a Mercy Seat for His glory. When He finds a house that has paid the price to build Him a resting place, He will stay. That is when we will see a revival that is unlike any we have ever seen before." [1]

This statement about the mercy seat intrigued me, and I began to dig deeper into the details of the Old Testament Tabernacle in search of the keys to revival. The Word of God is like a treasure chest with precious jewels waiting to be found.

As I studied the mercy seat, I started to learn where the focus of the church is to be. In Exodus, chapter 25, after giving Moses the Law, God commanded that a special dwelling place be erected for Him. Here His presence could be manifested daily, and here He could commune with the people through Moses and the high priests in generations to come. God has always wanted to dwell with man. He told Moses,

And there I will meet with thee, and I will commune with thee from above the mercy seat, from between the two cherubims which are upon the ark of the testimony, of all things which I will give thee in commandment unto the children of Israel.

Exodus 25:22

The glory of God would appear over the Tabernacle, and His presence would dwell between the mercy seat and the cherubim. This is a picture of what the Lord wants from His Church today—relationship with His believers, not the building.

Moses was first instructed to build the Ark of the Covenant out of acacia wood, and to overlay it with gold. This is symbolic of the perfection of Christ as He hung on the Cross. God told Moses to put the Ten Commandments inside the Ark—again pointing to the fact that Christ would come and fulfill the Law (Exodus 25:10-16).

Next, Moses was to make a mercy seat of pure gold (a type of the perfection of Christ). The mercy seat is the place of atonement (Exodus 25:17). It was exactly as advertised; it was a place of mercy.

God then told Moses to make two cherubim of gold, placing one at each end of the Ark. These represented the angelic beings who worship without ceasing in heaven. The Lord gave Moses some very specific details for making the cherubim. He said,

And the cherubim shall stretch out their wings above, covering the Mercy Seat with their wings, and shall face one another; the faces of the cherubim shall be toward the Mercy Seat.

Exodus 25:20

Notice that the Lord instructed Moses to have the cherubim facing each other, but their eyes were to be down, looking at the mercy seat where the blood was applied. Why? Because the center and object of our worship is Jesus Christ and His blood that was shed on the Cross. We are to be ever thankful for His blood that has cleansed us from all of our sins.

Two thousand years ago, Jesus Christ—the perfect Lamb of God, the perfect sacrifice—shed His blood on the Cross to appease or remove the judgment of God on a lost and sinful world. When a sinner comes to the Cross and puts his or her faith in what Jesus Christ did on the Cross to remove sin, God sends the Holy Spirit into the life of that person. This is the born again experience (John 3:3).

In fact, the discovery or revelation of the Cross as being the mercy seat is found in Romans 3:25, which says,

> *Whom God hath set forth* [Jesus] *to be a <u>propitiation</u> through faith in his blood, to declare his righteousness for the remission of sins that are past, through the forbearance of God.*

The word *"propitiation"* in the Greek is *"hilasterion,"* which means *"lid, covering, or mercy seat".* The truth of this scripture gives us an incredible revelation. Jesus Christ and Him crucified is the mercy seat. It was the mercy seat and the worship around the mercy seat, symbolized by the cherubim, that brought the glory of God.

When Jesus came up out of the water after being baptized by John the Baptist, the Bible says the heavens were opened and the Holy Spirit came down like a dove and landed on Jesus. And a voice from heaven spoke, saying, *"This is my beloved Son, in whom I am well pleased"* (Matthew 3:17).

God's favor rests completely on His Son Jesus Christ and what He did on the Cross. When the Church places Christ and His precious blood at the center of its worship, then and only then will the Holy Spirit descend and the favor of God be manifested. This is the key to seeing true revival come!

TRUE WORSHIP VERSUS FALSE WORSHIP

In recent years, there has been an incredible move of God in the area of worship. It has literally changed the Church world. This move of God is getting the bride ready for her Bridegroom. He is coming soon, and the Church of Jesus Christ is warming up for that awesome day when we will experience the pure worship in heaven with all the angels.

The Bible makes clear what the focus of worship is in heaven. It tells us that there are thousands and thousands of angels, living creatures, and the elders around the throne of God. They are all saying with a loud voice,

> *Worthy is the Lamb that was slain to receive power, and riches, and wisdom, and strength and honor, and glory, and blessing.*

Revelation 5:12

Further insight into the object of worship is found in the next verse,

> *And every creature which is in heaven, and on the earth, and under the earth, and such as are in the sea, and all that are in them, heard I saying, Blessing, and honour, and glory, and power, be unto him that sitteth upon the throne, and unto the Lamb for ever and ever.*

Revelation 5:13

All of heaven worships the Father who sits on the throne and the slain Lamb of God who is sitting at His right hand. They will be the object of our worship for all eternity. Notice the scripture refers to Jesus as the slain Lamb of God. This means that heavenly worship is in awe and appreciation for what Jesus Christ did on the Cross to redeem mankind.

The modern Church has, for the most part, left the Cross, and the center of worship today is not on the slain Lamb. Self and other things have become the objects of our worship. We must return to the ancient paths. Jeremiah the prophet said,

> *Thus saith the Lord: Stand ye in the ways, and see, and ask for the old paths, where is the good way, and walk therein, and ye shall find rest for your souls. But they said, We will not walk therein.*

Jeremiah 6:16

If we lose the focus of whom we are worshipping, then we are only offering false worship. The whole Tabernacle's focus was on the mercy seat. It was the place of atonement. It was the place where God would cover man's sin. The blood of the sacrifice had to be placed on the mercy seat on the Day of Atonement. This act of faith would appease the judgment of God toward the sins of the people.

When the Church takes its eyes off the blood and starts to look at worship—or anything else for that matter—it becomes false worship. The Apostle Paul understood what the central focus of the believer should be, and that is why he penned these words in 1 Corinthians 2:2,

> For I determined not to know anything among you save Jesus Christ and him crucified.

CHRIST AND THE CROSS ARE TODAY'S MERCY SEAT

When the Lord on Good Friday 1999 used that line from the movie *Field of Dreams*—*"If you build it, he will come"*—He in essence was saying, "I want you to build a Mercy Seat." The mercy seat is the Cross and the blood that Jesus Christ shed there. It should be the center of all worship. The "it" is Christ and Him crucified.

The Lord wants the blood of Christ clearly preached and taught in our churches. He wants us to understand that the Cross is for holy living (sanctification) just as much as the Cross is for salvation (justification). Divine healing comes through the Cross as well. (See Matthew 8:17.)

It is the desire of every true believer to have a divine encounter with God in which the Lord moves and speaks to us in such a way that we are changed forever. God wants to have a man encounter! He is just waiting for us to get our focus right.

When David returned the Ark to Jerusalem, he was in essence bringing back the presence of God that hovered over the mercy seat. David's main concern was not the gold box or even the Ten Commandments that were inside the Ark; he was concerned with getting the presence of God into the City of Jerusalem.

David's journey is a picture of the Church today. We are in need of seeing the presence of God come back to the Church. God has left most churches. He says to the Church of Laodicea in Revelation 3:20,

Behold, I stand at the door, and knock: if any man hear my voice, and open the door, I will come in to him, and will sup with him, and he with me.

This presents a very alarming visual. Jesus is outside of His Church, knocking on the door and trying to get in. What a terrible reproach on the Church of Laodicea! Unfortunately, this is the situation of many churches and many believers today.

Any time a church or a believer moves away from the Cross, you will find very little evidence of the Holy Spirit. You will only find spiritual barrenness. Most churches today have lost their way. Most (thank God, not all) are not preaching the Cross as they were 50 years ago. As a result, our Beloved has left the building.

I opened to my beloved; but my beloved had withdrawn himself, and was gone: my soul failed when he spake: I sought him, but I could not find him; I called him, but he gave me no answer.

Song of Solomon 5:6

REVIVAL IS COMING

I believe God is getting ready to again open the windows of heaven and pour out His Spirit just like He did in the Book of Acts. The question is, *"When and where will it begin?"*

The Church right now is like a woman who is nine and one-half months pregnant. The Church's belly is swollen, and we are uncomfortable. And like the expectant mother, we just want the baby to come out. There is a holy frustration in the hearts of many of God's people. We have heard about revival; we have read about revival. Some of us have even known elderly people who have lived through a revival, but most of us have never seen a true Holy Ghost revival.

We see the desperation of the world. We have experienced the dryness of the Church, and we are hungry for a move of God. It's the only answer for the backslidden Church.

I believe the Lord is rebuilding the mercy seat as the preachers and spiritual leaders of this land come back to the Cross. We need people like Martin Luther who will stand up and lead another spiritual reformation.

John Bunyan wrote a classic book called *Pilgrim's Progress* that has blessed millions, but he wrote another book that got less attention, *The Acceptable Sacrifice*. Bunyan wrote that he felt this was his best work—even better than *Pilgrim's Progress*. It was all about brokenness based on Psalm 51. He wrote: *"The costly key that unlocks the riches of God's presence is the brokenness of the heart towards what Jesus did on the Cross for us."* [2]

Christians around the world desire revival to come. For revival to be birthed, we must learn the lesson that David learned. In I Chronicles 13:7, we learn that they transported the Ark on an ox cart, but God had instructed them in His Word that the priests should carry the Ark. The Lord didn't want the strength of oxen to carry His presence; He wanted frail, pitiful men to carry it. He didn't want it to be easy; He wanted them to have to sweat and work hard to carry the Ark.

When seeking God for revival to come, things get heavier, not lighter. You sense the burden of lost souls, and it breaks you. Seeking God for revival will bring a demand of God for all flesh to die. It will be a painful journey, but in the end it will all be worth it. Most are not willing to pay this price. Most want an easy way, so they cram the holy things of God onto a new cart of man's making. They are more interested in the people being comfortable than they are in following God's Word.

Let me tell you, friend, God is not looking for the Church to have it easy, but He is looking to build His Church His way. And His way is the way of the Cross. The way of the Cross is not an easy way—in fact it is a narrow way, and most want to take the wide road. But if we will go the way of the Cross, which is to die to the flesh, then resurrection life will come. When new life comes, then the world will be changed. Glory to God!

WE MUST RETURN TO THE ORIGINAL PLAN

There is no new method or program that will lead us to revival. We need to rediscover God's original recipe and quit dabbling in producing new carts. The main thing the Church must do is make the main thing the main thing, and the main thing is Jesus Christ and Him crucified.

We must ask ourselves the question, *"Has the holiness of God changed since the days of the Old Testament?"* The answer is *"No!"* So why is there an attitude in the Church today that we can build new carts in the name of evangelism and it's okay? Why are we handling the things of God in an overly seeker-sensitive way?

Jesus said, *"And I, if I be lifted up from the earth, will draw all men unto Me"* (John 12:32). The Church today has become concentrated on drawing men instead of lifting up Jesus Christ and preaching the Message of the Cross. Our job is to lift up Jesus Christ and Him crucified, and His job is to draw the people. If the Church is built the way He tells us to build it, then He will come. And when He comes, then they will come!

My prayer is that everyone who reads *CrossEyed* will receive from the Lord a revelation of the Cross. However, if only one gets it, it was all worth it—even for just one!

NOTES

Chapter 3- The Sin Nature vs The Divine Nature

1. Wuest, Kenneth. *Romans in the Greek New Testament for the English Reader*, Wm. B. Eerdmans Publishing Company, Grand Rapids, MI, 1955, p.91

2. Ibid.

3. Wuest, Kenneth. *Romans in the Greek New Testament for the English Reader*, Wm. B. Eerdmans Publishing Company, Grand Rapids, MI, 1955, p.91, p 111

Chapter 4- How is the Sinner Saved?

1. Tozer, A.W. *Man: The Dwelling Place Of God*, Christian Publications, 1966, p. 72.

2. Robeck, Jr., Cecil M., *The Azusa Street Mission and Revival*, Nelson Reference & Electronic, 2006

Chapter 5- Why Am I Living The Defeated Christian Life?

1. Swaggart, Jimmy, SonLife Radio, Baton Rouge, Louisana

2. Ethics of America Youth, 2002 report (Marina del Rey, California: Josephson Institute Of Ethics, 2002)

Chapter 6- Fighting The Wrong Battle

1. Swaggart, Jimmy. *Expositor's Study Bible,* Jimmy Swaggart Ministries, Romans 7, p. 1981

Chapter 9- How Do I Walk In The Spirit?

1. Wuest, Kenneth. *Romans in the Greek New Testament* for the English Reader, Wm. B. Eerdmans Publishing Company, Grand Rapids, MI, 1955, p. 130

2. Ibid.

3. Wuest, Kenneth. *Romans in the Greek New Testament* for the English Reader, Wm. B. Eerdmans Publishing Company, Grand Rapids, MI, 1955

Cross-Eyed

Chapter 10- It's A New Day!

1. Wilkerson, David. *The New Covenant Unveiled,* Wilkerson Trust Publication, p. 54

2. Jimmy Swaggart Bible Commentary Volume One, World Evangelism Press, 1993, p. 189.

3. Wilkerson, David. *The New Covenant Unveiled,* Wilkerson Trust Publication, p. 57.

Chapter 12 - *"If You Build It, He Will Come"*

1. Tenney, Tommy. *God's Favorite House,* Destiny Image® Publishers, Inc., Shippensburg, PA, 1999, p. 49.

2. Bunyan, John. *The Acceptable Sacrifice*